REVISED EDITION

ASK
THE
RIGHT
QUESTIONS

HIRE
THE
BEST
PEOPLE

RON FRY

Best-selling author of
101 Great Answers to the Toughest Interview Questions

CAREER
PRESS

The Career Press, Inc.
Franklin Lakes, N.J.

ASK THE RIGHT QUESTIONS, HIRE THE BEST PEOPLE, REVISED EDITION

EDITED AND TYPESET BY KATE HENCHES

Cover design by Johnson Design

Printed in the U.S.A. by Book-mart Press

To order this title, please call toll-free 1-800-CAREER-1 (NJ and Canada: 201-848-0310) to order using VISA or MasterCard, or for further information on books from Career Press.

CAREER
PRESS

The Career Press, Inc., 3 Tice Road, PO Box 687,
Franklin Lakes, NJ 07417
www.careerpress.com

Library of Congress Cataloging-in-Publication Data

Fry, Ronald W.

    Ask the right questions, hire the best people / by Ron Fry. – Rev. ed.

    p. cm.

    Includes bibliographical references and index.

    ISBN-13: 978-1-56414-892-6

    ISBN-10: 1-56414-892-0

        1. Employee selection. 2. Employment interviewing. 3. Prediction of occupational success. I. Title.

    HF5549.5.S38F79 2006

    658.3′1124—dc22

2006022811

ASK
THE
RIGHT
QUESTIONS

HIRE
THE
BEST
PEOPLE

CONTENTS

Introduction

Green Light, Red Light

Nearly two decades ago, I wrote *101 Great Answers to the Toughest Interview Questions*. I hadn't been a great interviewee. Far from it—I had often *not* gotten jobs for which I was eminently qualified.

Despite my sterling reputation with employment offices, the book became a bestseller. In fact, it continues to sell, year after year. I don't pretend to know why it has done as well as it has, but I will hazard a guess: It's simple, straightforward, practical, and written in a welcoming and humorous style. (Okay, I suppose that counts as four and a half guesses.)

And it has clearly helped literally hundreds of thousands of candidates prepare for *you*.

The majority of my interviewing experience in the last decade has been on *your* side of the table—I've hired hundreds and interviewed thousands. Perhaps because I feel guilty for telling so many interviewees exactly what you want to hear, I thought it only fair that I help *you,* the interviewer, do a better job of finding the right candidates.

An organized layout to get you organized

Chapters 1 to 3 offer a detailed discussion of what you need to do and think about long before that cocky candidate chassé into the room—from writing cogent and effective job descriptions and ads to "buzzing" resumes, from types of interviewers to types of interviews, from how to handle a candidate who shows up an hour late to the "Silent Cal" and the "Verbose Victor." Interviewing may not be 99 percent preparation, but it may well be 50 percent. After you study the first three chapters, you *will* be prepared.

In Chapters 4 to 11, we'll get into the meat of the book—the questions you should ask and the answers you should expect to hear. (I have not counted the questions in this book, but there *are* more than the 101 I revealed to the candidates.) Additionally, I've laid out the book in a way that I hope makes it most practical and easy-to-use. Each question is usually followed by a series of three different subheadings:

What do you want to hear?
(What information should the question elicit?)

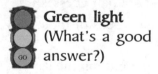 **Green light**
(What's a good
answer?)

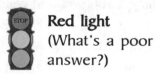 **Red light**
(What's a poor
answer?)

There may be follow-up questions or those you can substitute (variations) after each as well.

Red light means: Stomp on the brakes

I suspect the "red lights" after many questions will be the most-used part of the book, because they clearly indicate when you should hit the brakes and suggest the candidate hit the skids. These are answers that will make the average interviewer cringe and the busy interviewer suggest the candidate try another firm...right now, please.

After almost every question in the book, I could have included the same list of "general" red lights, those factors that should give you pause after any question...or in any interview. So as not to unnecessarily clutter up the book, let me just state these all-encompassing negatives right here:

Oh, did I forget to call?

Many interviewers will simply cancel (and not reschedule) an interview if the candidate is late. It doesn't matter that traffic backed up, his cat threw up a hairball, or he just got lost in the elevator.

Being on time is not racing down the final corridor with moments to spare. Some interviewers agree with football coach Tom Coughlin—if you're not 15 minutes *early,* you're *late.*

Nice hair...love the lipstick.

Poor grooming is a basic turn-off to most of us. I react negatively to candidates wearing too much perfume or cologne, more makeup than a runway model, an armload of bangles and bells, or sporting a 5 o'clock shadow...at 9 a.m.

First impressions *are* important and your initial gut reaction to a candidate *is* a valid one.

Uh, does that tie glow in the dark?

I was taught that a dark suit, pearls, and pumps is appropriate dress for female candidates. Given the tube tops, sneakers, short skirts, and patterned stockings I've seen waltz through my door (and all on one candidate!), some mothers have failed to teach their daughters similarly.

Men should wear a white or light blue shirt, conservative suit, silk tie, and shined dress shoes.

No matter how "loose" and unstructured your corporate culture, I would question the seriousness of a candidate sporting a tie that glows in the dark or a T-shirt advertising anything (but especially not anything X-rated!).

Are you a tobacco farmer?

Even if you are a smoker, your company may be wary of hiring a candidate who smokes at all—let alone during the interview—because of the additional health risks (and costs) he brings to the table. You cannot summarily declare such a candidate *persona non grata*, but his smoking may well be a factor you consider.

Of course, if a candidate decides to smoke during the interview itself—and some have in my office—you can encourage her to go down to that front door right away to finish up.

You brought your cat. How nice.

There should be a new reality series featuring the bizarre behavior of some interviewees, as they chew, burp, scratch, swear, cry, laugh, and scream their way into our hearts. Interviewees have shown up drunk or stoned, brought their mothers with them, fallen asleep, even gone to the bathroom and never returned.

Keeping a cell phone on during the interview qualifies as inappropriate behavior. Actually receiving or making a call ranks as bizarre.

You will not be blamed if you wonder, "If this is her *best* behavior, what (*gasp!*) do I have to look forward to?"

You don't need a lie detector.

Checking references is vital. While some candidates have always "fudged" their credentials here and there, the number of candidates who brazenly lie about where and when they worked, what they did, and/or where and when (or even if) they attended college, has skyrocketed. One resume-writing service estimated that nearly half of the resumes they vetted contained serious inaccuracies.

No matter how lowly the job, there are significant expenses involved with hiring someone to perform it, so you must take the time to check out references. And the higher up on the food chain the job is, the more intensive your scrutiny must be. The CEO of Radio Shack and the chairman of Bausch & Lomb both recently resigned after claiming fictitious college degrees.

Lacking a particular skill or experience may not automatically exclude someone from getting the job. Lying about it should.

I don't need you to be *that* honest.

While honesty may be the best (and only) policy, you may be taken aback if a candidate is a little *too* confiding—anything he does in the privacy of his own home is not something you need to hear.

Some candidates will make your job decidedly easy because of their tendency to blurt out the truth. When I asked one woman what interested her about a job opening, she responded, "Heck, I just need a job with benefits. I owe way too much on my Visa."

"Last job? Hated it!"

A candidate should attempt to make every minute of his interview a positive experience. In my mind, someone who complains about his last job, boss, duties, or even the elevator ride upstairs is not someone *I* want to hire. Which is why *you* may want to introduce negativity, just to see how he handles it.

Uh, look over here please.

To many interviewers, a candidate's inability to "look them in the eye" indicates he has something to hide, as does being overly fidgety or nervous. You should expect a promising candidate to greet you with a firm handshake, sit straight up, and, of course, look you in the eye.

Likewise, you should be seeking people who are enthusiastic about what they do, so a candidate who sighs, looks out the window, or checks her watch during an interview may not fit the bill.

Study the candidate's "body language." While many people don't mean what they say or say what they mean, their nonverbal actions reveal *exactly* what they're feeling. According to studies, *more than half* of what we are trying to communicate is being received nonverbally.

She might be a trifle *too* confident.

A candidate once said to me, barely five minutes into our interview, "I've got three other offers right now. What can you do for me?"

I showed her the door.

Yes, you are seeking confident, enthusiastic, and cheerful (and brave and clean and reverent...) candidates, but be wary of those who are too "over the top."

"Uh, why do you want to know?"

If you ask a simple question and a candidate starts to sweat, hem and haw, and try to change the subject, you are free to wonder what she is hiding. Because if she isn't hiding anything, why is she acting so defensively?

"What does this company do?"

A key part of the interview process is preparation—researching the company, industry, and position, preparing pertinent questions, and nimbly sprinkling that knowledge into the conversation. So you should seriously question the commitment of a candidate whose questions or answers clearly indicate a lack of such preparation. I *have* had candidates ask me what exactly my company did.

The answer: Not hire *them*.

"Sure, Bob, you can have the lobster."

An interview over lunch is an excellent way to get a candidate to reveal aspects of his personality or behavior you want to know about, even if it's just whether Mom taught him manners. An otherwise attractive candidate may seem decidedly less so after blithely ordering the most expensive item on the menu or inelegantly slurping spaghetti or soup.

"And then I worked for...oops!"

Throughout this book, I have attempted to give you the ability to formulate questions to elicit what you *really* want to know. The best answers are those that are most responsive to your stated (or unstated) needs. Because these answers should be "customized" to "mesh" the candidate's qualifications with your company's needs, it's often difficult, if not impossible, to say that a particular answer is "right" or "wrong." But there are answers that *are* clearly wrong:

- ☞ Any answer, no matter how articulate and specific, that fails to actually answer the question asked.

- ☞ Any answer that reveals that the candidate is clearly unqualified for the job.

- ☞ Any answer that provides information that doesn't jibe with a candidate's resume and/or cover letter. (Don't laugh. I, for one, have proudly given details about a job I did not include on my resume. The interviewer didn't laugh either.)

- ☞ Any answer that reveals an inability to take responsibility for failures/weaknesses/bad decisions/bad results, or that tries to take full credit for a project to which others clearly contributed.

Although you may not consider any of these an automatic reason for immediate dismissal, an accumulation of two or more should give you pause. (And some, of course, like dishonesty, should make you do more than just pause.)

Setting up your interview plan

The questions in this book are grouped by type. They are not in some suggested order. Many of the questions in Chapter 10, for example, may be some of the first questions you ask in every interview! So read the entire book and then decide, on a case-by-case basis, which questions to ask (and in what order) as you approach each candidate. And don't forget Chapter 11, which covers the illegal and ill-advised questions. You don't want to ask them!

Finally, a word about the usage of gender throughout this book. Instead of being gender-biased, I've chosen to split the difference and mix up the usage of "him" and "her" wherever it doesn't get too cumbersome.

Rather than spend a lot more time telling you what you're going to learn, let's just get you started. Good luck.

Ron Fry
September, 2006

CHAPTER ONE

INTERVIEW PREPARATION

Interviewing?" you chortle. "It's a snap—I just do it by instinct. Place an ad, attract some applicants, get acquainted, ask them a few questions, then hire the person who seems least likely to blow up in my face (or the one I can get for the least amount of money). What's the big deal? This isn't rocket science, you know."

Well, okay, if that's what you think works for you. But does it really?

Or, as I suspect, do you find yourself interviewing for the same position every few months because you insist on "doing it by instinct." In which case, all you're doing, by instinct or otherwise, is wasting your time.

Some interviewers fool themselves into believing that they can improvise their way to a successful hire with little or no preparation. I don't think you can. The cost of hiring an employee today is staggering, and poor hires have a way of affecting the careers of the managers responsible for them. That means *you*.

The hard truth is that hiring the right person for the job takes a lot of work, both before and during the interview. It is not just a function of asking the right questions *during* the interview, but also spending the time to prepare *before* the interview. Although such preparatory work is not that difficult to complete, my sense is that it's routinely ignored by a majority of employers, especially small company managers. Such interviewers "wing it"—and then wonder why the person they hired either didn't work out or quickly left to take advantage of another opportunity.

What is this job, anyway?

You'll find it difficult to evaluate applicants, much less attract and retain good people, if you haven't established a clear and concise set of requirements for the job. In this chapter, you'll learn how to:

- ☞ Develop a working job description that makes sense to your organization—and to prospective employees.
- ☞ Compose and place a winning ad that will attract the most-qualified applicants.
- ☞ Evaluate resumes effectively and efficiently.

Identify and define the position you need to fill

Is your organization experiencing high turnover in a particular position? If so, it's entirely possible that the job is poorly defined or that the components of the job description are totally incongruous. (Another possibility, of course, is that you have *no* written job description for employees to use as a starting point, in which case you should expect continued personnel headaches.)

One entrepreneur I know told me of a job she once tried to fill whose duties included the following:

- ☛ Conducting regular meetings with key vendors.
- ☛ Evaluating quotes and references from new vendors.
- ☛ Making critical marketing strategy recommendations.
- ☛ Managing the inventory in a 5,000-square-foot warehouse.
- ☛ Composing initial drafts of flyer and catalog copy.
- ☛ Analyzing cash-flow predictions.
- ☛ Filling in for telemarketing staff when absences arose.

Do you see a problem here? Six different hires in an equal number of months certainly did. The longest lasted two months; the shortest (smartest?) two days.

The various elements of the job were so wildly out of balance (and required such varied skills and training) that no one person could have ever reasonably been expected to fulfill all of them. As a result, no matter how accomplished a new hire, he or she quickly felt overwhelmed, overworked, and underpaid.

One of the initial keys to hiring the right person for the job is to make sure it is *a* job, not a series of disparate tasks that would tax Michelangelo's spectrum of skills.

You know and I know that there are times when a dynamic company needs to ask employees to "pinch hit" in areas outside their daily routine. But there has to *be* a daily routine from which to deviate! Before you try to find the "perfect person" for your "perfect job," take a long, hard look at exactly what that job will mean to the person who will spend the majority of his or her waking hours performing it.

If your job offers no defining, consistent sense of purpose, you will find it very difficult to attract an applicant who will perform it well over an extended period of time. Remember: "Revolving door" positions cost your company money! In most workplaces, asking the company "Renaissance person" to sweep up or punch endless reams of figures into a computer system is an expensive mistake that will inevitably leave someone (probably you) in permanent "search mode."

Remember: They are not you

Here's an important reminder for entrepreneurs and others who have personal stakes in their organizations: *You* may well be willing to wake up early, stay late, and do anything—repeat, *anything*—to ensure the attainment of your company's goals. You may *have* to scrub toilets *and* crunch numbers *and* pack shipments *and* make sales calls *and...and*.... But you chose the bed—you have to make it, sleep in it, and pay for it.

As a fellow entrepreneur, I applaud your dedication, zeal, and crazy (and totally unsupported) belief that you will, of course, defy all odds and actually succeed.

At the same time, you should be aware that the rest of the working world may not share your willingness to "go the extra mile" day in and day out.

If you want an accountant, create a job description that focuses on accounting work. If you want a salesperson, the job description should focus on sales work. If, however, you want someone who will pay any price as an accountant, bear any burden as a salesperson, and share your personal willingness to peel dried chewing gum from beneath tables at 11 p.m. on a Saturday night, you're going to have a problem. You're not looking for an employee; you're looking for a kindred spirit. You may have to wait awhile before you find one. And, when you do, you may well have to give up a piece of your company to compensate him or her for the overweening dedication you expect.

Some companies develop cogent-seeming job descriptions that include an innocent-sounding catch phrase: "other duties as required." Then the poor new hire comes to realize that 85 percent of the day consists of tasks that fall into that "other duties" category. Save yourself—and your employees—some aggravation. Make sure the "miscellaneous" category in the job description does not camouflage something an otherwise qualified person would reasonably resent doing—or feel frustrated enough about to consider parting company.

Take a long look at exactly what needs doing. Identify irrelevant components of the job. Then be honest about what should stay in the job description and what should be reassigned to someone else. You should share your conclusions with others in the organization and get their input. Don't stop lobbying until you've developed a workable job description that's both coherent and well-organized around a central theme. Remember: The fact that you are (or would be) willing to perform any given task in the description will not be persuasive to an employee who ends up feeling pulled in 16 different directions. Make it your goal to avoid hiring applicants who (secretly) plan to stay with you only until a better opportunity arises.

Next, do a little brainstorming about the background, experience, and skills your ideal candidate should bring to the table. Try using the following questions as a starting point:

- What kind of educational background is required?
- What level of computer experience is required?
- What specific software tools are required?
- What other technical skills are required?
- What business background should the applicant have?
- What communication skills are required to fulfill the tasks associated with this position?
- How important are problem-solving skills in this position?
- What kinds of day-to-day challenges will the successful employee need to routinely overcome?

The classified advertisement on page 23 is a good example of a well-thought-out job description.

Pay particular attention to the specificity of each of the job duties listed.

DISPLAY DESIGNER
(reporting to Head of Product Design)

The Display Designer will:

- Understand perspective drawing, vacuum forming, injection molding, and fabrication.

- Utilize both two-dimensional and three-dimensional software to develop new product designs.

- Generate concepts for complex projects, drawing on a working familiarity with materials and processes within our overseas manufacturing facilities.

- Travel occasionally to our overseas manufacturing facilities to oversee initial production runs and troubleshoot manufacturing problems.

- Work with marketing team to develop competitive products; assist in critique of marketing plans and campaigns.

- Meet at least weekly with the head of the Design Department to provide updates on current projects.

- Attend occasional seminars and personal development programs within the field, under the guidance of the head of the Design Dept.

- Attend goal-setting events, as well as quarterly and annual departmental training sessions.

The Display Designer should possess a college degree and at least two years of related computer design work experience. Exposure to process engineering and manufacturing issues is a definite plus.

As you work to develop and refine the job description, remember this old punch line: "Forgive me for writing you such a long letter, but I didn't have time to write a short one." Many applicants and employees are so intimidated by long job descriptions that they never read them all the way through. Make sure yours are both comprehensible and concise. Yes, it may take time (and, in larger organizations, a certain amount of political skill) to finalize a cogent, powerful document that captures all the essentials of the job. This will, however, be time well spent.

Think of it this way: If you don't work with the people in your organization to devise a job description that clearly sets out a range of related, interconnected responsibilities, you will almost inevitably end up hiring someone who abandons your organization the moment a better opportunity comes along. A "hit-and-run" hire will cost your company money, and it certainly won't reflect well on the person who interviewed the fast-disappearing candidate! Yes, that person would be you.

Ideally, your job description should outline duties that will match up closely with the life and career goals of a particular applicant—the right applicant. For instance, after reading the sample job description on page 23, an applicant who's hoping to grow in the computer-aided design field and gain some exposure to the world of marketing would probably be motivated by the brief outline the company prepared. On the other hand, the same applicant would probably be cynical indeed after reading a job description that made it clear that the company expected some strange hybrid of Leonardo da Vinci, Zig Ziglar, and the King of Queens to show up for work every day.

Remember that people work for a number of reasons, not just money. Job satisfaction is a big part of the equation. Personal rewards and fulfillment must be taken into account, and the requirements of the job must be perceived as congruent, tangible, and realistic by job seekers and employees alike. Ask yourself: Will the person *want* to fulfill the requirements of the position you've designed? Why?

Regardless of the level or nature of the position, a well-focused job description proves to the applicant that someone has taken the time to actually think about what needs to be done and who is needed to do it.

Writing an ad to attract the right applicants

In a perfect world, simply mentioning your job opening to a few close friends and/or trusted professional colleagues would result in all the resumes you needed to conduct an effective search. Alas, we don't live in a perfect world. Word of mouth can and should be part of your campaign, but, in most cases, composing and placing some sort of classified ad should be, too. (I'm assuming here that you aren't paying an executive search firm or other service to conduct the search for you.)

Anyone who's ever run a classified ad in a newspaper can share a story of being deluged with calls, letters, even unannounced visits from eager (and, all too often, supremely unqualified) applicants. Although there's probably no way to avoid the headaches associated with wading through the correspondence and calls that follow an ad placement, you can improve the likelihood that your ad pulls in the kinds of applicants you want.

Here are six ideas that will help you to do just that:

[1] Choose your headline carefully

I once saw a classified ad whose headline read, "Workers Wanted." What a waste of space! Most employers opt to identify the title of the position in the heading. That's fine—but what *else* could you say in that headline? Consider the following:

Telemarketers (Experienced)

Telemarketers: We Want the Best—and Pay the Most!

Which one would *you* find more persuasive if you were an ace phone salesperson looking for a better outfit?

[2] Use "enhanced excluders"

A well-constructed job description should give you a clear idea of the kinds of skills and experience that are essential to that job. Highlight them in your advertisement, and don't be afraid to emphasize them. If your gut feeling is that the job requires two years of experience, what's wrong with asking for three years in the advertisement? You'll get a higher grade of queries, and the few people who do contact you with only two years of experience are likely to be more motivated than the average applicant.

"Enhanced excluders" point you toward the "high end" of the applicant pool; they allow you to set the bar *slightly* higher than you need to. You can always ignore the standards you've set for the right candidate. Frankly, it can be quite interesting to see which applicants try to get around your announced requirements...and how compelling a case they can make for themselves. In the end, of course, the choice of whom to interview is yours, regardless of what you put in the ad.

[3] Specify the technical skills you need

If candidates absolutely, positively, *have* to be proficient in PageMaker 7.0 or some other computer software, feature that requirement prominently and specifically in the advertisement. This sounds self-evident, but you'd be surprised at the number of hiring managers I've spoken to who don't specify particular skills they're seeking—and then complain about the experience levels of the candidates they interview.

Ambiguous statements like "good computer skills" aren't sufficient. Briefly state *exactly* what technical skills you want (and, if space allows, how the skills will be put to use) within the ad.

[4] Give applicants a sense of your "corporate culture"

Is your organization a creative new startup? An industry leader? A nonprofit organization with a sense of mission that all its employees share? Paint a brief portrait of your company, and let your readers know into what kind of culture they'll be asked to fit. This really can make a difference in the quality of applicants you attract.

Similarly, you should make an effort to give the reader some sense of what the daily routine is likely to look and feel like. Is the environment fast-paced? Is quality control an obsession for people in this department? Are you looking for someone who brings a high level of creativity to the workplace? Use another sentence to let the reader know whether his or her working style and outlook on life will be valued and rewarded at your organization. (If you're comfortable including salary ranges, feel free to do so.)

[5] Be creative in selecting advertising media

The Sunday edition of your local paper may be a great place to run your ad. However, if you're searching for someone with a highly technical background, it may not be. Consider listing such an opening in industry trade journals, with local college and graduate school placement offices, professional and/or trade organizations, on the Internet, or a combination of these outlets.

The Web can be a particularly effective (and afford-able) way to reach out to qualified applicants whose com-puter literacy is more or less guaranteed. What's more, the era when this medium could only be relied upon for the recruitment of technical people, such as computer program-mers, has certainly passed. Many industries have associations that feature job openings on their Websites, and, of course, there are the broad-based sites such as Monster or Career Builder.

[6] Avoid public employment services

At the very least, use such agencies to circulate your ad only when you're filling extremely low-level positions. Yes, they're free. And yes, it would be won-derful if they worked. As much as I'd love to recommend state unemployment offices as primary resources for the recruitment of superior candidates, I really can't. The bad reputation these institu-tions have earned among employ-ers is, for the most part, well deserved.

Unless you're trying to fill a bottom-of-the-ladder position that requires little or no computer literacy or any other marketable skills, the odds are that you'll save a lot of time and effort circulating your advertisement elsewhere. There's no percentage in screening more unsuitable applicants than you absolutely have to, is there? On page 28 is an example of an ad that works.

Note the inclusion of the phrase "We are an equal opportunity employer" or the letters "EOE" near the end of the ad. In our lawsuit-happy era, you should take every opportunity to reinforce the message that your organization plays fair and square when it comes to hiring.

What to look for in the resumes you receive

You've told everyone you know about the kind of employee you're seeking, composed a killer ad, and placed it in front of the right audience. Your campaign has produced a flurry (or blizzard?) of resumes.

Now what? How on earth do you turn that overflowing pile of self-aggrandizement into a small, manageable selection of top-tier candidates, one that showcases the few, the proud, and the highly qualified?

Step one is to review the job description you composed earlier. Refresh your memory. Go through the list of requirements you established. Remind yourself which elements you considered absolutely essential. Then "buzz" those resumes.

That's right—I said "buzz" them, not "read" them. One of the most enduring fictions of the world of employment is that prospective employers are under some moral compunction to actually read every stultifying word of the resumes they receive. Nothing could be further from the truth.

A resume is a document prepared for the employer's convenience. As far as you're concerned, it has one purpose and one purpose only: to make it easier for you to remove people from consideration. So if you've established that strong writing ability and a familiarity with PageMaker 7.0 are vital requirements for the job you're trying to fill, you're going to hurtle through that pile of resumes and look for 1) evidence of writing ability, and 2) the word "PageMaker." Resumes that pass your test stay "in." Resumes that fail are "out."

Are you feeling guilty about being so ruthless? Over the years, more than a few people have told me that they actually feel obligated to read vast piles of resumes without screening them in the way I've just outlined. They feel that they're not giving applicants or their own organizations a fair shake unless resumes receive a word-for-word, line-by-line analysis. To such hardy souls I can only pass along three brief observations:

1. Time is a precious gift.
2. Our Creator has blessed us with a limited amount of it.
3. It makes no sense to squander that gift exploring the syntax of an applicant who has given no evidence of minimal fitness for the job.

Make no justifications. Buzz the resumes and *instantly* reject those that do not meet your basic standards.

As you conduct this initial screening maneuver, you'll be able to remove from consideration a large chunk of the resumes on your desk—typically between 50 and 80 percent of them. You'll also find that something very interesting takes place. Of the resumes that remain, some will make a much more positive impression on you than others. There are two likely reasons for this.

First, the applicant may have taken the time and trouble to compose the resume and cover letter specifically to fit the opening you've advertised.

Second, the applicant may have work or educational experience that is particularly appropriate—a potential sign of a good match that "jumps out at you."

Place a small check mark in the upper-right hand corner of any resume that catches your eye for either of these reasons.

What have you accomplished so far? You've used your time very wisely by "buzzing" the resumes into an "in" pile and an "out" pile, and by placing a small check mark on resumes in the "in" pile that made an instant, positive first impression on you. Now that you've done all that, put the stacks of resumes away and do something else for a while. You want to clear your head so you can give all your attention to the very best candidates in the pile. Give yourself a break of at least a couple of hours before you review the "in" pile again.

When you start your review, you'll want to look at each resume a little more closely than you did the first time through. Read each resume once, and make notes in the margins as you go along.

What exactly are you looking for as you do this more detailed read-through? Beyond the formal requirements of the job, you want applicants whose resumes demonstrate confidence, enthusiasm, experience, and dependability.

Here's a strategy you can use to identify those qualities. Focusing only on the resumes in your "in" pile, and focusing *first* on the resumes that bear a check mark, *add* one check mark to the resume you're reading for every "yes" answer you can give to the questions that follow.

A word of caution, however: Be sure to apply the questions to both the resume *and* the cover letter. Many exceptional candidates will use the cover letter to amplify relevant experience. Reading the cover letter carefully may also give you immediate exposure to communication strengths (or weaknesses) that are not immediately evident in the resume.

☛ *Does the applicant make reference to at least one relevant success story that matches the requirements of the position, as you've identified them?* Past success in a similar situation indicates a good chance of success in the position you're trying to fill.

☛ *Do the person's qualifications mirror the background of an employee who has performed at a superior level in this position?* A profile that matches up favorably with that of a top performer in your organization is worth reviewing closely. Keep an eye out for parallel educational accomplishments, similar career progress, even comparable leisure avocations that support workplace performance, such as involvement with Toastmasters International or a professional association.

☛ *Do educational and/or training credentials appear to be above average for this position?* Consider not only prestigious colleges and grade point averages, but also any references to professional seminars, workplace training, and other signs of commitment to personal and professional development.

☞ *Is the sequence of jobs or study clear and comprehensible, with no unexplained employment/education gaps during the previous five years?* Some resumes are designed to emphasize relevant skills and experience over chronology. This can make it difficult to evaluate the person's recent career path and overall dependability. If a candidate's resume has effectively camouflaged his recent past, but you want to interview him anyway, be sure to ask for a detailed, chronological work history early on. Be wary of unexplained gaps.

☞ *Is the resume and/or cover letter impressively creative or unusually well-executed?* People who go the extra mile to win your attention in a tasteful and compelling way may be above-average problem-solvers. Give them credit for innovation in the face of the problem "How do I make this resume memorable?" They may well take a similarly resourceful approach to other problems that come their way.

Now make an X in another corner of the correspondence for every "yes" answer to the following questions. Again, be sure to consult both the resume *and* the cover letter:

☞ *Are there obvious typographical or grammatical errors?* If the applicant can't be bothered to spell your name or your company's name correctly, or to appeal to someone for help in constructing a coherent sentence, there could be a problem with attention to detail in a work-place setting. Don't underestimate the importance of care and accuracy in this area. Given the availability of computerized spell-checkers and the incessant urging of innumerable career counselors, articles, and books never to send out a resume or cover letter unless a third party has read it for errors, there's simply no excuse for such sloppiness.

☞ *Does the applicant use the resume or cover letter as an opportunity to complain or assign blame— for anything?* This can be a very dangerous sign. Beware of applicants who won't make the effort to approach challenging situations optimistically when constructing their resumes or cover letters.

☞ *Are any of the applicant's claims obviously over-stated?* People who stretch the truth on their resumes and cover letters will probably stretch the truth in other situations. There's a difference between putting the best possible "spin" on an experience and outright lying. If you know or strongly suspect that the person's resume contains a statement that falls into the second category, "X" it.

☞ *Is the resume itself difficult to follow?* Resumes and cover letters are miniature tests of one's ability to convey important information concisely and effectively. If the document fails the test, "X" it.

Once you've asked each of these questions about all the resumes and cover letters in your "in" pile, you should have a group of resumes with checks and X marks on them. Then:

- ☛ Take any correspondence that has *even one* X mark and place it in your "out" pile for now. You can always reevaluate your decision later. At the moment, your aim is to focus on candidates whose credentials and presentation are exemplary.

- ☛ Take any correspondence that has no marks whatsoever and place it in a new pile, your "backup" pile. These are people you may choose to contact later if your top choices don't pan out.

- ☛ Take the remaining correspondence and place it in descending order, with the candidates who have the most check marks at the top of the pile.

Congratulations! You already know whom you want to interview. What form should that interview take? And how should you initiate contact with the applicant?

You'll find those answers in the next chapter.

CHAPTER TWO

SORRY, YOU'RE *NOT* READY TO START INTERVIEWING

Now that you have a group of first-tier applicants and a backup group of second-tier candidates, it seems like it's time to take action—to call all the top people and ask them to swing by for an in-person interview. Right?

Wrong!

Before you make those calls, you should have a clear understanding of the dominant interviewing styles, the pros and cons of each, what kind of preparatory work precedes an effective contact with a prospective employee, and what basic interview strategies there are to choose from. In this chapter, you'll learn about all these areas.

Your dominant interviewing style

Odds are that you are already inclined to one of three predominant interviewing styles: the "Telephone Screener," the "Human Screen," or the "Manager"—thanks to a combination of personal temperament and (you guessed it) your role in the organization and your daily workload.

Review the following profiles closely. I believe you'll find that you already instinctively favor one of these three approaches over the other two.

The "Telephone Screener"

As we'll see a little later in this chapter, telephone screening is an effective tactic used by many interviewers in all three categories. People in this first group, however, rely on the strategy as a *primary* means of exploring employment possibilities. For many of these interviewers, the in-person interview is little more than an opportunity to confirm what they feel they've already learned on the phone.

Interviewers who typically fall into this category are entrepreneurs, CEOs, high-level executives, and others short on time and long on vision. Their guiding philosophy could be summed up as: "My time is at a premium, I have a personnel problem to solve, and I don't plan to waste my valuable time talking in person to anybody but the very best."

The Telephone Screener is often the dominant interviewer at small- to mid-sized companies where no formal human resources (or personnel) department exists or where such a department has only recently been created. The primary objective of the Telephone Screener is to *identify reasons to remove the candidate from active consideration* before *scheduling an in-person meeting.*

Among the common reasons for abrupt removal from the Telephone Screener's short list: evidence that there's a disparity between the resume and the person's actual experience; poor verbal communication skills; lack of required technical skills.

The "pros" of this style

These interviewers are focused, efficient, and direct. Their no-nonsense approach often results in comparatively rapid hires. The time advantage on a personal basis is obvious—anyone who's ever handled a day or two of interviews knows that a single in-person visit with an applicant can eat up an hour or more of a workday with startling ease.

Telephone Screeners tend not to waste much time interviewing mediocre applicants. Their approach and overall interview philosophy may well be the best for the "emergency opening" situation—those times when the organization has lost a key player and must replace the person more or less instantly.

The "cons" of this style

Telephone Screeners may sometimes be too focused on short-term outcomes for their own good. For instance, they may not be in the best position to take advantage of the strengths a given candidate could bring to a position other than the one that's momentarily captured their attention. Because they're often acting in response to a single pressing need within the organization, they may not always pick the best candidate for long term growth.

As noted earlier, many Telephone Screeners are entrepreneurs and presidents of companies who conduct extensive (and often dazzlingly effective) phone interviews, confirm their own instincts with a single in-person meeting, then hire someone on the spot. This may intimidate or alienate other members of their team, notably Managers, who have been given no chance to evaluate the applicant as a potential colleague or subordinate.

The "Human Screen"

Many human resources and personnel professionals fall into this category. For these people, interviewing is not simply a once-a-quarter or once-a-month event, but a key part of their daily job description. They meet and interview many people, and are more likely than either of the other two categories to consider an exceptional applicant for more than one opening within the organization.

A primary objective of the Human Screen is to *develop a strong group of candidates for Managers to interview in person.* To do this, of course, they must fend off many applicants and callers—a daunting task, because the Human Screen or the department in which he or she works is often the only contact provided in employment advertisements.

Among the most common reasons for removal from the Human Screen's "hot" list are: lack of formal or informal qualifications as outlined in the organization's job description; sudden changes in hiring priorities and personnel requirements; poor performance from the applicant during the in-person interview itself; and inaction due to the Human Screen's uncertainty about the applicant's current status or contact information. That last reason is more common than other interviewers might imagine. If you're a Human Screen, you already know the feeling of helplessness associated with being constantly swamped with phone calls, resumes, and unannounced visits from hopeful applicants. Odds are that you also know that, despite your best efforts, you sometimes lose track of qualified people.

The "pros" of this style

Human Screens excel at separating the wheat from the chaff. Because they are exposed to a wide variety of candidates on a regular basis, they usually boast more face-to-face interviewing experience than members of the other two groups. Human Screens may be more likely to spot inconsistencies or outright lies on resumes, simply because they've seen so many over the years that they know when a candidate's credentials for a given position don't quite pass the "smell test."

And although interviews with Telephone Screeners or Managers may be rushed to accommodate hectic schedules, Human Screens are generally in a position to spend a comparatively long amount of time with a particularly qualified candidate. That means they're often more likely to find a larger number of potentially strong matches than members of the other two groups.

The "cons" of this style

These interviewers often do not have direct knowledge of the day-to-day requirements of the job to be filled. They have formal summaries, of course, but often don't possess the same firsthand familiarity with the skills, temperament, and outlook necessary for success on the job. Typically one step away from the action, they're reliant on the job postings and experience summaries composed by Managers.

If those formal outlines are imperfectly written, and if Human Screens receive no direct input from supervisors on the kinds of people they're looking for, the applicants passed through the system may well be off the mark.

Not surprisingly, Human Screens often react with a puzzled look when asked by others to offer their "gut reaction" on the merits of a particular candidate. Because they're generally operating at a remove from the work itself, they often prefer quantifying their assessments of candidates in hard numbers: Either the candidate *does* have three years of pertinent experience, or she *doesn't*. Either she *has* been trained in computer design, or she *hasn't*. Of course, this analysis may overlook important interpersonal issues.

The Manager

This category describes supervisors who choose (or are required) to fit in-person interviews into their busy working days. Typically, they are interviewing applicants they themselves will oversee; frequently, the interviews are the result of referrals from a Human Screen, or from colleagues and personal contacts.

The primary objective of the Manager is to *evaluate the skills and personal chemistry of the applicant on a first-hand basis.* These interviewers want to get to know everything they can about the people with whom they'll be working closely.

Common reasons for being dropped from the Manager's "hot" list include: lack of personal chemistry or rapport with the Manager; poor performance during the interview itself; and the Manager's assessment that the applicant, though qualified and personable, would not fit in well with the team.

The "pros" of this style

Often, these are the people with direct supervisory experience in the area in which the opening has arisen. A Manager who has worked with a number of previous employees who held the same position brings an invaluable level of experience to the proceedings.

Such interviewers often have an excellent intuitive sense of who will (and won't) be likely to perform the job well and achieve a good "fit" with the rest of the work group. What's more, Managers are usually in an excellent position to provide an applicant with immediate exposure to the other members of the team with whom they will be working.

The "cons" of this style

It sometimes comes as a surprise to applicants that excellent supervisors can be less than stellar interviewers, but a great many Managers lack any formal training in the art of interviewing.

Of the three categories, this is the group most likely to (mis)use the interview as an opportunity simply to "get to know" more about the applicant—rather than to identify specific answers to important questions about the person's background, experience, outlook on work, and interpersonal skills.

Another problem is that Managers, like Telephone Screeners, are often pressed for time.

Effective screening techniques

Whichever interviewing style you favor, you should be aware that simply calling all the people in your pile of top-tier resumes to set up an appointment is likely to be a waste of that most precious resource: time. Many applicants are skillful writers (or know skillful writers who are willing to prepare resumes and cover letters for them). Often, however, the person presented to you on the sheet will not match up with the flesh-and-blood human being it purports to describe.

Before you make the investment in time and energy to meet with anyone face-to-face, call and chat. Give yourself the chance to evaluate the confidence, enthusiasm, experience, and dependability of your most promising leads. You should do this even if you're not a Telephone Screener by nature.

If you're committed to using your time effectively, then you are obliged to regard the initial call as a screening interview, rather than simply a means of setting an appointment. For this interview (in fact, for *any* employment interview), you should be prepared to ask four types of questions:

1. *Rapport questions.* These are questions that allow you to build interpersonal bridges with the candidate. They typically occur early on in the discussion and are meant to encourage the candidate to feel comfortable with you and, by extension, with your company. ("Hi, Bob, how are you doing today?")

2. *Open-ended questions.* Questions that allow the candidate a great deal of leeway in describing what he or she does best. ("Can you tell me about a time when you were really proud of what you did at Acme Company?")

3. *Probing questions.* These questions focus on particular skills related to a specific workplace experiences or decisions. ("Can you tell me specifically what steps you took after the blackout to make sure that every department was prepared for a future emergency?")

4. *Questions that aren't questions.* This is your chance to put the candidate at ease by giving gentle but clear instructions, rather than asking pointed queries. It takes some practice, but it's very effective at getting candidates to open up. ("What would help me most would be to learn what you felt was your most important experience as a young stockbroker. Please take a moment and think of

an event from your early years at Cadwell House that you feel shaped your career in an important way. When you're ready, share that experience with me.")

The opening of your phone screen could sound like this:

You: *Mike Jones?*

Applicant: *Yes?*

You: *Hi, Mike. This is Mary Sweeney at Consolidated Widgets. You'd sent your resume over to us last week in response to our ad for a widget inspector. That's the ad that ran in the* Sunday Independent-Journal*?*

Applicant: *Oh, right, right...*

You: *I was hoping I could talk to you for a few minutes. I'm glad we were able to connect.* (rapport question) *How are you?*

Applicant: *I'm fine. I'm really happy you called!*

You: *Well, that's great to hear. I hope I haven't caught you at a bad time.* (rapport question) *Have you got a few minutes right now, or should we schedule another call? It's fine if you want to set up another time.*

In most business settings, this is regarded as an extremely weak way to open a conversation, because it leaves the other person a clear opportunity to say, "Actually, I'm right in the middle of something just now." In this setting, however, that's exactly what you want to do: give the other person an opportunity to get off the phone.

Some applicants are so nervous during an unexpected call from a prospective employer that their responses will be virtually meaningless. They need a chance to get their bearings. By opening the conversation in this way, you give the candidate a chance to soothe the butterflies that may have suddenly taken up residence in his stomach. Be prepared to schedule another time or, at the very least, give the applicant a moment to track down that resume, take a deep breath, and make a good impression.

The applicant will either suggest setting up a new time to talk with you, or suggest that the conversation continue. Whichever the case, you'll want to continue the phone interview with a little small talk, then move directly into a few basic questions to get a better sense of what motivates the person you're talking to:

You: (rapport question) *So you live in Cambridge?*

Applicant: *Yes, I've been here for about eight years now.*

You: (rapport question) *Do you have an apartment there?*

Applicant: *Yes, right off Central Square, next to the super-market. Do you know the area?*

You: *I sure do. As a matter of fact, about three years ago, I had an apartment myself in Harvard Square, on Bow Street. I guess that's about 10 minutes away.*

Applicant: *Oh, yeah, I know where that is.*

You: *Well, Mike, I wanted to get in touch with you because we've been looking at a lot of resumes, and yours stood out from the pack. I was wondering if I could ask you a couple of questions about your work history?*

Applicant: *Great, go ahead.*

At this point, you'll want to pose some preliminary questions and *take written notes of the answers you receive.*

Remember that your aim is to identify candidates who possess the requisite skills *and* demonstrate confidence, enthusiasm, experience, and dependability. Following are some examples of the kinds of questions you should consider posing during a telephone interview. (You can conduct a more extensive phone interview by using the questions that appear later in this book.)

Open-ended question: *What do you enjoy most about working as a ____?*

Open-ended question: *What do you like least about it?*

Probing question: *Think of a specific time when you faced a challenge in the area of ____. Can you tell me what steps you took to overcome that challenge?*

Question that isn't a question: *It would really help me to have some idea of what prompted you to apply for this position, and how you see it fitting into your career growth. Please take a few moments to go over how you decided this job could be a good fit for you, what interested you most about our company, and what kind of salary level you think is appropriate for someone with your experience.*

You should also feel free to ask for clarification of anything that seems unclear to you in the person's resume. For instance, if the person spent a particularly long time in a given position, you might ask what made him or her decide to stay there for so long.

Do not ask about the candidate's age, ethnic origin, marital status, religious beliefs, family status, social availability, sexual activities or sexual orientation, either directly or indirectly. Posing questions such as these is an excellent way to invite a lawsuit against your organization. Ask *only* questions that will help you determine the candidate's ability to effectively perform the duties you require. (See Chapter 11 for a more detailed discussion of illegal and ill-advised questions.)

During the call, listen for responses and stories that showcase the applicant's confidence, enthusiasm, experience, and dependability. Remember that people who like what they're doing tend to do a better job. This is not to say that everyone you interview must spout mindless good cheer at all times. But you do want to keep an ear out for applicants who sound engaged, intelligent, and motivated throughout the conversation. After all, that's how you want them to show up Monday morning!

Listen for indications that the person has already done some kind of research on your organization. This shows initiative and speaks well of the candidate's organizational skills. These days, it's so easy to conduct a search on the Web that I suppose employers should probably be dubious of any applicant who *doesn't* attempt to research the company.

Steer clear of the candidate who habitually focuses on negatives or appears eager to assign blame to colleagues, family members, or supervisors. As someone who has conducted a fair number of telephone interviews, I can assure you that it's surprisingly easy to determine from a single phone call if someone holds a basically cynical view of life.

Consider asking for the names of references you can call, and be suspicious if none you can actually speak to are forthcoming. I recently heard of an applicant who passed along to prospective employers an impressive list of references, all of whom happened to be out of the country and inaccessible for some months. It turned out (surprise, surprise) that the candidate was camouflaging some very serious deficiencies in his job history.

Be wary, too, of candidates who go out of their way to share carefully crafted malicious accounts of experiences with past employers or who volunteer information that is clearly confidential. The phrase "accident waiting to happen" should come to mind when you encounter such applicants.

The telephone interview you conduct can be as long or as short as you feel appropriate. The main rule to follow is *not* to extend an offer for a face-to-face interview to an applicant whom you feel is not well-suited to the position or your company. If the phone interview has led you to this conclusion, there are two ways to wrap up. The first is probably the easiest. You simply say something like this:

Mike, I really appreciate your taking the time to talk about your background with me today. You've given me a lot to think about. You should know, though, that this is a very competitive position, and that we'll be talking to a lot of people over the next week or so. I think the way I'd like to leave this is that if we feel there's the possibility of a good match for this position or for any other opening, we can get back in touch with you at this number. Does that make sense?

This allows you to exit the conversation gracefully, without deflating the person's ego too much—and without burning bridges unnecessarily. After all, if another position comes up for which this person *is* perfect, you *do* want to be able to get in touch!

There is another school of thought about the best way to conclude a conversation with someone who does not meet your standards for the open position. It's the direct approach—which I personally favor:

Mike, I've listened carefully to what you've told me today, and I have to be honest with you—I don't think we have a good match here. We're going to have to take a pass this time around.

Whichever approach you decide to use, bite the bullet and conclude the conversation *without* setting a time for a face-to-face interview with this person. It simply doesn't make sense for either of you to commit to a time-consuming, in-person meeting if you already suspect the candidate is under-qualified, hostile, uncommunicative, or in any way a bad choice for the position.

If, on the other hand, you decide after your initial telephone interview that it makes sense to meet with this person, go ahead and set the date.

Regardless of whether the call went well or poorly for the applicant, you should record your impressions of the call right away. Immediately after you've concluded the call, write down a few sentences summarizing your reactions to the applicant, as well as the reasons you decided to pursue further discussions—or not to. The way you initially assess an applicant's phone performance can be a good signal of how the person will interact with you or others in the workplace.

In our litigious age, it's an unfortunate fact that you must protect yourself from disgruntled job seekers who file suits alleging illegal discrimination. That's why it's a good idea to record the legal and legitimate reasons for your rejection of a person's candidacy. Make note of answers that left you cold. Briefly jot down the details of those elements of the person's background or work experience that seemed to you to represent a poor fit with the position.

On a less ominous note, you should specify in your notes how you felt about each of the people whom you *did* schedule for an interview. Was the chemistry between the two of you favorable? What memorable comments did the person make? What was the candidate's general level of knowledge about your industry and the likely day-to-day duties of the job?

What made you decide to meet with this person? Was it the applicant's poise and unflappability? Her mastery of technical details? Her knowledge of your company's products and services? The initiative she showed in asking you to meet with her personally?

I know of a sales manager who never hires a salesperson unless he or she directly and clearly asks for an appointment or a job offer. He makes a habit of not calling candidates back after he interviews them. He's waiting for them to "ask for the order"...by asking for the job!

If you're not interviewing someone for a sales position, that's a fairly aggressive stance to take. I would, however, make note of all those applicants who take the bull by the horns and say something like, "I'm very excited about this opportunity and would like to start working for you" somewhere along the line. Such applicants should be given serious consideration—they are committed to making something good happen.

Take detailed notes, including, of course, any questions or reservations you have concerning the person's candidacy. These notes will be invaluable later on in the process, when you must consider each of the candidates individually before making a hiring decision. (Of course, you also should take plenty of notes during your face-to-face interview, and, in the same way, summarize your reactions briefly at its conclusion.)

Types of interviews

There are a number of styles and guiding philosophies when it comes to person-to-person interviews. The overall goal, of course, is to screen out applicants who lack the aptitudes (and attitudes) you're looking for, and to keep talking to only the most promising people.

Although experienced interviewers may use more than one strategy, it's essential to know which mode you're in at any given point—and why. Here's a summary of the methods and objectives of the most common approaches.

The behavioral interview

In this format, your conversation with the candidate will focus on his or her past experience. You're hoping to learn more about how he or she has already behaved in a variety of on-the-job situations. Then you'll attempt to use this information to extrapolate the person's future reactions on the job.

How did the person handle himself in some really tight spots? What kinds of on-the-job disasters has he survived? Did he do the right thing? What were the repercussions of the decisions he made?

You're not looking for perfection, but rather for a thorough understanding of what happened and why in a given workplace situation, and what was learned as a result. Beware of applicants who claim that they've never made mistakes or never found anything new to learn from a challenge. You're trying to ensure the candidate can actually "walk the walk," not just "talk the talk." You want to hear specific examples of problems he faced, the actions he took, and the results he achieved.

The team interview

In many organizations, a team of three or more employees may interview an applicant for an open position, either separately or together.

The team interview can range from a pleasant conversation to a torturous interrogation. Typically, the applicant meets with a group of interviewers around a table in a conference room. A variation that's less stressful for the candidate involves a "tag team" approach, in which a single questioner exits and is followed by a different questioner a few minutes (or questions) later. (For the latter approach, it's essential to set up a coordinated strategy ahead of time, so as not to subject the applicant to the same questions four or five times in a row.)

The team members who take part in a group interview may be members of the department in which the candidate would work, or they may be a cross section of employees from throughout the company. Whichever approach you take, there should be some format for a group discussion of the candidate's pros and cons *shortly after the interview takes place.* Ideally, you'll want to compare notes immediately after the group interview so as to record impressions while they're still fresh in everyone's mind.

As you discuss the results of a team interview, you'll want to consider each person's assessment of the candidate's suitability and experience. Ask about any instances that showed a candidate's lack of respect for the various members of the team. Did the candidate dismiss out of hand the concerns of an administrative or support employee who was on the team? Was there a lack of respect for the organization's policies and procedures? Did the candidate treat every member of the team with respect and deference?

The team interview is a great way of minimizing the risk associated with the ever-more-expensive challenge of making the right hire. With more than one set of eyes and ears assessing the candidate, there's less chance you'll settle on the wrong person. Just be sure to canvas each member of the group and discuss all concerns openly and fully once the interview is complete. There's no point in going to the (sometimes significant) logistical trouble of scheduling a team interview if you're not going to elicit and record all of the feedback...or ignore it.

The stress interview

Formal qualifications are important, but in some jobs, the emotional demands, sudden emergencies, and breakneck pace of work can be downright intimidating—not once in a while, but every day. Even a candidate who knows all the technical moves may wilt under the glare of an etiquette-challenged boss or crumble when inheriting a surrealistically compressed deadline.

When you're hiring for such positions—whether you're looking for a stockbroker, an air traffic controller, or a prison guard—it may not be enough to ascertain that the candidate is capable of performing the job under the *best* conditions. You may well have to find out for sure how the person will do under the very *worst* conditions. And that's where the stress interview comes in.

The stress interview is designed to cut through all the pleasantries and get right to the heart of the matter. A common enough question in this setting could sound gruff or rude—which is exactly how it's *supposed* to sound. Rather than a pleasant, "So, tell me about yourself," a stress interviewer may snarl (literally), "So, why the hell should I hire *you* for anything?"

Here are some techniques stress interviewers have been know to use:

> ☞ He ridicules everything the candidate says and questions why she's even interviewing at his company.

☞ She says nothing when the candidate enters the room…and for five minutes afterwards…then just stares at the candidate after he answers her first question.

☞ He keeps the candidate waiting past the scheduled time and then keeps looking at his watch as she answers questions.

☞ She stares out the window and seems to be completely uninterested in everything the candidate has to say.

☞ He challenges every answer, disagrees with every opinion, and interrupts the candidate at every turn.

☞ She doesn't introduce herself when the candidate walks in, just hits him with a tough question.

☞ He takes phone calls, works on his computer and/or eats lunch as he interviews candidates.

☞ She may seat candidates in a broken chair, directly in front of a high-speed fan, or next to an open window…in the dead of winter.

The point of a stress interview is not to take pleasure in another human being's discomfort, but to find out exactly how the person responds in a tough situation. Does the candidate maintain eye contact? Take a few seconds for a deep breath? Keep a level and professional tone of voice? Ask for more information? If so, you may have found someone who can take the heat.

But do yourself and the job seekers of the world a favor: Save the stress interview for candidates who really are being considered for extremely demanding positions. Otherwise, the kind of treatment cited above will just earn you and your company a reputation as an uninviting sweatshop.

(Don't confuse a stress interview with a *negative* interview, which is sometimes an effective technique. In the latter, the interviewer merely stresses the negative aspects of the job at every opportunity. He may even make some up—"Would you have any problem cleaning the toilets every Saturday morning?" or "Will three hours of daily overtime be a problem for you?" It still may be an unpleasant interview for a candidate, but it isn't a sadistic one.

The case (situational) interview

"You're dealing with a publishing client. His printer just called and said the biggest book of the year had a typo on the spine. A bad typo. More than 100,000 books have already been printed. What should he do?"

If you are working at a consulting firm, law firm, or counseling organization, you probably are used to conducting this type of interview.

Responses to hypothetical questions can give you an invaluable look at someone's values, thinking processes, and practical experience. That's why situational interviewing has become so popular in recent years.

The premise is sound: Present the candidate with situations that might, hypothetically, occur on the job in order to gauge the degree to which he or she demonstrates the traits for success. It's hard for an interviewee to prepare ahead of time for these questions. That means you get to watch the person try to analyze an unfamiliar problem and develop a strategy to solve it, on the spot. Take notes on what happens after you ask a situational interview question. (It's almost always interesting.)

What you want to hear should ideally be a combination of real-world experience, inspired creativity, and the willingness to acknowledge when more information or assistance is in order. (Many interviewers pose hypothetical questions designed to smoke out people who find it impossible to reach out to other team members for help.) Does the person plunge right into the situation or take the time necessary to offer a reasoned, intelligent response to the question you've posed?

Situational interviews help you identify people who can step back, weigh the alternatives, and choose the best course of action. Just remember that technical skills are not all you're measuring. A highly skilled computer programmer, for instance, may constantly sow discord in the workplace or abuse rules concerning tardiness. You're interested in someone who not only *can* do the work, but also *will* do the work—and contribute as an effective, motivated member of the team.

(While case interviews are geared to upper-echelon candidates, applicants for many different kinds of jobs may be given the opportunity to show what they can actually do on the job: Clerks may be given typing or filing tests; copy editors given minutes to edit a magazine article or book chapter; a salesperson may be asked to telephone and sell a prospect; or a computer programmer may be required to create some code.)

The brainteaser interview

As Microsoft interviewers have famously been known to ask, "How would you move Mt. Fuji?" The list of questions designed to assess how *creatively* an applicant approaches a problem—as opposed to the logical approach case interviews are designed to highlight—are virtually unlimited:

☞ How many oil wells are there in Texas?

☞ How many dentists are there in Poland?

☞ How would you build a better mousetrap?

These types of questions are particularly useful when interviewing someone for either a highly creative position or one that requires superior analytical skills.

The hiring interview

Though some strategies are more popular than others, many savvy interviewers consider all of the types of interviews you've just explored to be effective ways to get an understanding of what makes a candidate tick during an early face-to-face meeting. Once you bring someone back for the second time, however, the stakes are considerably higher. You have to decide whether or not to hire that candidate. An approach that at least includes, if not features, a team interview is highly recommended during this second level of interviewing.

Sadly, this advice is rarely implemented in today's workplace. A common (and often ill-fated) approach is for an experienced Human Screen to handle the initial interview, and for a Manager (typically the hiring manager) to conduct the next discussion with the applicant in a one-on-one setting. The problem is that many managers lack formal or informal training in conducting interviews of any kind. As a result, quite a few are just as nervous as the job seekers they're interviewing. Is it really that surprising that, left to their own devices, they don't always make the best hiring decisions?

If you're a hiring manager who must evaluate a candidate during a hiring interview, my advice is threefold:

First, finish reading and re-reading this book from cover to cover.

Second, set up a *written* interview outline ahead of time. In other words, don't wing it. Decide what you want to learn about this applicant and which questions from this book's successive chapters will help you get the information you need.

Finally, get other team members involved in the interview process, and compare notes before you make a final decision.

One last piece of advice on the mechanics of the hiring interview: You'll no doubt be talking to multiple applicants, looking for that unique blend of confidence, enthusiasm, experience, and dependability that screams "hire me." It's quite common, however, to find yourself looking at two or more applicants who display such traits in abundance. All other factors being equal, you'll want some kind of tie-breaker prepared.

One of my favorite tie-breakers is to ask an applicant what books, courses, or seminars have helped him or her onto a path of personal self-improvement—and when. The more responsibility someone has demonstrated for his or her own personal growth, the more credit they get in my book. The more frequently a person tries to learn about how to be a happier, more productive, better-balanced person, the more I want that person on my team.

Now that you've got a sense of what the interview process feels like, how can you be sure you're effectively evaluating all the information you'll be receiving from all those enthusiastically motivated, top-tier candidates you've found?

That's what you'll find out about in the next chapter.

Chapter Three

Preparing for the Answers to Come

E ffective interviewing requires both listening and observational skills. Tone of voice (including verbal timing) and body language play incredibly important roles in human interaction. In fact, it's been estimated that 93 percent of what actually influences people is attributable to factors *other than* the *literal* content of the words they hear.

It follows, then, that the words a candidate uses to respond to you during an interview are barely a corner of the picture he or she is painting for you. In this chapter, I'll give you some powerful tools for interpreting the *non*verbal messages you receive from the job candidates you interview. I'll also cover some common occurrences—if a candidate is late, won't talk, or won't shut up—and give you some general guidelines for handling them.

What to look for: The initial greeting

When you first encounter the candidate, silently ask yourself questions like the ones that follow. The more often you can answer yes, the more likely it is that you've been blessed with a poised, confident candidate. Of course, no one is suggesting that confidence and social grace can compensate for lack of ability in the workplace. But in a perfect world, wouldn't you prefer to work with someone who meets all of the formal qualifications *and* has enough self-confidence to interact well with others?

☞ Did the candidate grip your hand firmly, avoiding both the "bone-crusher" and the "wet fish" approach?

☞ Did the candidate shake your hand with purpose?

☞ Did the candidate hold the shake for an appropriate period, neither too short nor too long?

☞ Did the candidate use one hand? (A two-handed shake is usually regarded as a sign of over-familiarity at the outset of the first meeting, though there are some regional/cultural exceptions to this rule.)

☞ Did the candidate look you in the eye?

☞ Did the candidate smile?

☞ Did the candidate use your name when greeting you?

What to look for: Body language

Once the candidate takes a seat, you'll be doing the lion's share of the talking to begin the meeting. This is when the person is likely to be the most nervous, and when rapport-building questions (see Chapter 2) will be most welcome. *After* you have put the person at ease by asking a few such questions, begin to monitor his or her gaze, physical posture, and general bearing. Use the questions below as a rough guideline, and take discreet notes as the interview moves forward. The more "yes" answers you record, the more comfortable (and, presumably, forthcoming) the person is likely to feel interacting with you.

- ☞ Does the candidate make appropriate intermittent eye contact with you—neither staring you down nor avoiding your gaze?

- ☞ Is eye contact broken only at natural points in the discussion, rather than suddenly, as in the middle of an exchange?

- ☞ Is the candidate's mouth relaxed? (A tightly clenched jaw, pursed lips, or a forced smile may indicate problems handling stress.)

- ☞ Is the candidate's forehead and eyebrow area relaxed?

- ☞ Does the candidate occasionally smile naturally?

- ☞ Does the person avoid nodding very rapidly for long periods of time while you're speaking? (This is shorthand for "Be quiet and let me say something now," and it is inappropriate in an interview setting.)

- ☞ Does the candidate move his or her hands so much or in such a weird manner that you actually notice? (Constant twitching of the fingers—or even worse, knuckle-cracking—may mean you're dealing with a person who simply can't calm down. Yes, an interview is an unsettling experience, but so are some of the tasks this person will have to perform on the job!)

- ☞ On a similar note, does the candidate avoid shuffling and tapping his or her feet?

☞ Is the candidate's posture good? (Chair-slumpers send a silent message: "I'm not even trying to make a good impression." If you hire them, you may encounter that message on a daily basis.)

☞ Are the candidate's eyes gazing forward, rather than darting all over the room?

☞ Is the candidate's head upright?

☞ Does the candidate tend to sit with crossed arms? (This may signal either a confrontational attitude or a sense of deep insecurity, neither of which is a great sign.)

☞ Does the person appear to be breathing regularly and deeply?

☞ Is the person's personal hygiene and grooming acceptable? (Would you want to sit next to this person during a long meeting? Ask yourself: If the candidate won't make an effort to clean up his or her act for a job interview, what will an average workday be like?)

What to listen for: Length, tone, and timing of responses

What the candidate says is certainly important, but so is *how* he or she says it. Take circumspect written notes if you cannot answer yes to all of the following questions during the interview. Three or more such notes during the course of the interview should raise questions about a candidate's social skills.

☞ Does the candidate respond in a clear, comprehensible, and confident tone of voice?

- Does the candidate avoid prolonged pauses in sentences?

- Is the candidate's speaking rhythm consistent and totally appropriate?

- Does the candidate avoid rambling answers?

- Does each of the candidate's answers have a concluding point or do they seem to trail off into nothingness?

- Does the candidate avoid interrupting you? (Breaking in while a prospective future employer is speaking shows poor judgment and underdeveloped people skills.)

- Does the candidate take time to consider difficult questions before answering them?

- Does the candidate ask for additional information or clarification when dealing with complex questions?

- Does the candidate offer answers that are consistent throughout?

As you monitor nonverbal signals during the interview, bear in mind that physical actions and vocal delivery should support the answers the interviewee passes along. A candidate who assures you that he has what it takes to survive the ups and downs of a career in sales, but looks pale and shell shocked when you mention that you're interviewing other candidates, is sending two very different messages. The "lyrics" may be saying "I can handle rejection," but the "music" doesn't quite support that contention!

What if the candidate shows up late?

A candidate who is even modestly prepared will usually be sure to arrive at your office 15 minutes early, to "get the lay of the land," freshen up, and calm down. Even if the unexpected pops up—an accident occurs, the baby gets sick—a responsible candidate will do one of three things:

☛ If he's on his way and will be slightly late, he should call (I sometimes think I'm the only person in the world who manages to exist without a cell phone).

☛ If she's allowed enough extra time, she may deal with the unexpected and still arrive on time. If she's smart, you won't even know anything untoward has occurred. (Why introduce a negative into the conversation?) A savvy candidate should have scouted your location already and prepared alternate routes if she anticipates traffic snarls.

☛ If it's impossible to make the appointment at all, a good candidate will call you at least 15 minutes beforehand to explain what went wrong and attempt to reschedule. It's up to you how you respond to such a phone call. My personal take is that accidents and emergencies do happen and, as long as I'm notified beforehand and not two hours after the fact, I tend to give candidates the benefit of the doubt.

What if you never get a phone call and the candidate is significantly late? I would consider it a mark against him, especially if he fails to bring it up or sufficiently explain his reasons for the lateness. (Despite the usual advice to "avoid negatives" in an interview, this just begs for an explanation, and not offering one is a bigger negative.)

What if the candidate spouts generalities?

It's up to you to ask the probing questions necessary to translate some of a candidate's repetitive adjectives—"hard-working," "responsible," "loyal," "creative," and so on—into specific examples that demonstrate the experience you're seeking.

This may be due to simple nervousness or be evidence that there are very few specifics to talk about! Keep probing and, if necessary, use their resume to guide you: "I notice on your resume that you worked at Acme Co. for two years in the marketing department. What specific projects did you work on?"

If necessary, you may have to come right out and put her on notice that you need more than generalities on which to base a decision: "I appreciate your self-evaluation and I'm sure you are hard-working, intelligent, and so on, but I need you to tell me some specific examples from your work experience that illustrate those traits."

If, despite your best efforts, you still get little or nothing, you probably need to assume that the candidate has added a bit of fluff to the resume and is having a hard time giving you specifics...because they just don't exist.

What if you catch the candidate in a lie?

I doubt there's anyone out there who hasn't attempted to make a lowly, repetitive job sound a bit more glamorous and responsible than it really was. Or someone who "forgot" to put a short-term job on their resume and extended their stay at another by a month or two to cover it up. And I would take such "little white lies" with a grain of salt.

However, a truly blatant lie—claiming to have worked at a company when he didn't, altering a job title, vastly exaggerating duties and responsibilities, lying about her salary history, claiming a college degree that doesn't exist—is, to me, a clear reason to end the interview without further ado.

What if the candidate is silent?

There are shy people and there are those who become overly nervous during the interview process, no matter how nice and inviting you are as an interviewer. What do you do when the person in front of you seems to be applying for the position of "clam"?

Thinking or acting impatiently will most likely exacerbate the situation, turning a nervous candidate into a potentially comatose one! Let him know that you appreciate that the artificial nature of the interview can make some people overly nervous. Encourage him to take a couple of deep breaths. Smile, relax, and urge him to relax. And if it doesn't work? Ask whether he would like to reschedule for another time.

What if the candidate talks very little?

There may be an occasion or two during the interview when you receive a brief, seemingly content-free answer along the lines of "I don't know" or "Sure, all the time" or "When there were problems, I sat down with people and worked them out." When this happens, you will want to try to draw the person out by asking a relevant probing question as a follow-up: "Can you give me a specific example that would show me what happened when you took that approach with a coworker?"

If the probing question results in another curt non-response, guess what? This person is not playing ball with you. Proceed with caution. The interviewee may be hiding something or have sub-par communication skills.

What if the candidate won't shut up?

You smile and say, "So, tell me a little about yourself," and before you know it, 10 minutes have elapsed and he's barely out of elementary school! Perhaps he's just a talker, or maybe his verbal diarrhea is the way he responds to an attack of interview nerves. In either case, it's your job to handle his verbosity.

Make your questions as focused as possible so as to encourage equally focused responses. If the candidate still believes the journey to the end of the interview should explore every highway and byway along the road, take every opportunity to insert a new question into any pause.

What if nothing you do can blunt the verbal assault? I would ask myself whether such talkativeness will harm the environment for others (to which the answer would probably be a resounding "yes"), then let him talk his way into some other company.

What if the candidate is obviously under- or overqualified?

If the candidate's experience, education, demeanor, and behavior clearly bear as much resemblance to the job as I do to Mel Gibson, you'll want to save the time and energy of continuing an interview that will clearly end up in a terse letter of rejection. Cut your losses early, and let the candidate know that the skills and experience she has simply don't match those of the job. Be polite, be nice, but be firm and move on to a more qualified interviewee.

On the other hand, an obviously overqualified candidate may present you with different options. He may be completely wrong for this job but perfect for another, unadvertised position in your area. He may be a great candidate for a job with another department or division. She may be a candidate to keep on file for a job opening that occurs in the future (presuming you're impressed by her demeanor, behavior, and so on). Or, and this depends very much on your own circumstances, she may still be a candidate for this position because of her own situation. And, because of her obvious overqualification, she may be far more valuable even in the short term than a more "perfect" long-term candidate. If an overqualified candidate is willing to make a commitment—six months minimally, perhaps a year—and to take the high end of the salary offered but not more, you may be better off hiring her for the short term.

You've done the up-front work. You're ready to move on. In the chapters that follow, you'll find the actual questions that will become the heart of your interview plan.

CHAPTER FOUR

HOW TO KEEP THEM TALKING

B ob thinks he's a pretty good interviewer. He has a list of 15 questions he asks every candidate—same questions, same order, every time. He takes notes on their answers, even asks an occasional follow-up question. He's friendly, humorous, excited about working at Netcorp.com. As he tells the candidate...in detail...for *hours*. Then he wonders why only a small fraction of his hires pan out.

The purpose of the interview is to get the *candidate* talking, and talking, and talking. I'm sincerely happy you like your job, admire your boss, and love your company. But don't let this adoration lead to an interview in which you talk three times more than the interviewee!

I've never really understood the interviewer who thinks telling the story of his life is pertinent. Why do some interviewers do it? Part nervousness, part inexperience, but mostly because they have the mistaken notion they have to sell the interviewee on the company, rather than the other way around. There *are* periods, instances, and reasons why this *may* be necessary—periods of low unemployment, a glut of particular jobs and a dearth of qualified candidates, a candidate who's so desirable you know you have to outsell and outbid your competition for his or her services. But don't make it a rule to turn the interview into a sales conference. Under most circumstances, let the candidate do the talking—and the selling—and sit back and decide if you're ready to buy.

What's ideal? I doubt there's a definitive answer or one based on any systematic study, so I'll just lay out my own opinion: If you interview someone for an hour and spend more than 15 minutes talking yourself, you're letting *them* interview *you*.

The more you find yourself blathering on about the wonderfulness of everything from the cafeteria to your newly acquired file cabinet, the less likely you are to ask the open-ended, probing questions you need to identify the right person for the job.

So make it a habit to ask beautifully broad, open-ended questions at the start of every interview. Get them talking, and keep your own tongue on a leash.

Q: So, tell me a little about yourself.

This question is your icebreaker. It gives you a chance to gauge initial chemistry, get a little insight into the cipher sitting before you, and makes *them* do all the talking for at least a couple of minutes!

Should this time-tested question catch them unprepared? Certainly not. Every interview book I've ever seen (or written) has pretty much guaranteed that this will be one of the first three questions asked, often the very first one!

What if they do hem and haw their way through a disjointed, free-associating discourse that starts somewhere in Mrs. Korbut's kindergarten class and, 10 minutes later, is just getting into the details of those 8th grade soccer try-outs? You just tied the record for the shortest interview of the week. Thank them and move on to the next candidate.

What do you want to hear?

It's just a starting point, but you want a well-thought-out, logically sequenced summary of the candidate's experience, skills, talents, and schooling. A plus? If this tightly focused introduction (of about 250–350 words) clearly and succinctly ties the candidate's experience into the requirements of the position. So a smart interviewee should have prepared an "opening statement" that consists of:

- ☞ Brief introduction.
- ☞ Key accomplishments.
- ☞ Importance of these strengths and accomplishments to you, the prospective employer.
- ☞ Where and how the candidate sees himself developing in the position for which he is applying (tempered with the right amount of self-deprecating humor and modesty).

Green light

So many books (including mine) have touted proper preparation for "Tell me about yourself" that it's probably the most rehearsed answer you'll get. If you're lucky, you'll hear something like what Barb, a recent college graduate applying for an entry-level sales position, said:

"I've always been able to get along with different types of people. I think it's because I'm a good talker and an even better listener. (Modestly introduces herself, while immediately laying claim to the most important skills a good salesperson should have.)

"During my senior year in high school, when I began thinking seriously about which careers I'd be best suited for, sales came to mind almost immediately. In high school and during my summer breaks from college, I worked various part-time jobs at retail outlets. (Demonstrates industriousness and at least some related experience.) *Unlike most of my friends, I actually liked dealing with the public.* (Conveys enthusiasm for selling.)

"However, I also realized that retail had its limitations, so I went on to read about other types of sales positions. I was particularly fascinated by what is usually described as consultative selling. I like the idea of going to a client you have really done your homework on and showing him how your products can help him solve one of his nagging problems, and then following through on that. (Shows interest and enthusiasm for the job.)

"After I wrote a term paper on consultative selling in my senior year of college, I started looking for companies at which I could learn and refine the skills shared by people who are working as account executives. (Shows initiative both in researching the area of consultative selling to write a term paper and in then researching prospective companies.)

"That led me to your company, Mr. Sheldon. I find the prospect of working with companies to increase the energy efficiency of their installations exciting. I've also learned some things about your sales training programs. They sound like they're on the cutting edge. (Gives evidence that she is an enthusiastic self-starter.)

"I guess the only thing I find a little daunting about the prospect of working at Co-generation, Inc., is selling that highly technical equipment without a degree in engineering. By the way, what sort of support does your technical staff lend to the sales effort?" (Demonstrates that she is willing to learn what she doesn't know and closes by deferring to the interviewer's authority. By asking a question the interviewer must answer, Barb has also given herself a little breather. Now the conversational ball sits squarely in your court.)

Based on the apparent sincerity and detail of her answers, it's not a bad little "speech" of a mere 253 words, is it?

With nearly a decade of experience in his field, Ken is applying for his dream job as a district general manager for a firm that provides maintenance services to commercial and residential properties.

Going into the interview, he knows he has a couple of strikes against him. First of all, he's already held four jobs, so he's moved around a bit. And he doesn't yet have the management experience required by the job—virtually the equivalent of running a business with revenues of $7 million a year.

But because he has anticipated what might otherwise have been a devastating first interview question—"Tell me something that will help me get a better feel for you than what I get here on the resume" (a nice variation on "Tell me about yourself")—Ken is prepared with this winning counterpunch:

"I'm a hard worker who loves this business. I've been an asset to the employers I've had, and my experience would make me an even greater asset to you.

"I think these are the most exciting times that I've ever seen in this business. Sure, there's so much more competition now, and it's harder than ever to get really good help. But all the indications are that more and more companies will outsource their maintenance needs and that more two-income households will require the services that we provide.

"How do we get a bigger share of this business? How do we recruit and train the best personnel? Because they are, after all, the secret of our success. Those are the key challenges managers face in this industry.

"I can help your company meet those challenges. While resumes don't tell the whole story, mine demonstrates that: I'm a hard worker. I've had promotions at every company I've worked for.

"I would bring a good perspective to the position because I've been a doer, as well as a supervisor. The people who have worked for me have always respected my judgment, because they know I have a very good understanding of what they do.

"And I have a terrific business sense. I'm great at controlling expenses. I deploy staff efficiently. I'm fair. And I have a knack for getting along with customers.

"I've always admired your company. I must admit I have adopted some of CleanShine's methods and applied them in the companies I've worked for.

"I see now that you're branching into lawn care. I worked for a landscaping business during my high school summers. How is that business going?"

In a mere 278 words, this successful candidate managed to:

☞ *Focus you only on the positive aspects of his resume.* Sure, he has changed jobs. But after this answer, you're likely to think, "Gee, look at all he's managed to accomplish everywhere he's been."

☞ *Get the interview started in the direction he wants it to go.* He demonstrated leadership abilities, experience, and a good understanding of the market.

☞ *Introduce just the right amount of humility.* While taking every opportunity to turn the spotlight on his many accomplishments and professional strengths, Ken portrays himself as a roll-up-the-sleeves type of manager who will be equally at ease with both blue-collar workers and the "suits" back at headquarters.

☞ *Turn the interview back over to you by asking a very informed question.*

Although both Ken and Barb rehearsed their speeches, neither memorized them word for word. Ken additionally sprinkled in a little industry jargon here and there, which was entirely appropriate.

Red light

☛ *Lack of eye contact.* You're asking this question to get a little chemistry, and so far the candidate hasn't conjured up a reaction.

☛ *Lack of strong, positive phrases and words.* It's the first question and, therefore, the first chance for the candidate to get off on the right foot. Shouldn't you be expecting words that convey enthusiasm, responsibility, dedication, and success? If the very first answer is uninspired (especially an answer we all assume has been prepared and even rehearsed), I have almost never seen the interview improve very much. Cut your losses and move on.

☛ *A general, meandering response that fails to cite specific accomplishments.* It's a plus if the candidate has been savvy enough to "edit" what we all know is a well-rehearsed set speech to ensure that it's relevant to the job at hand. Shouldn't you consider it a minus if all you've heard is a bunch of generalities with few or no examples to back them up?

☛ *No relevance to the job or your company.* Some candidates believe this question is an invitation to tell you about their hobbies, pets, favorite ice-cream flavor, or boy band. You may give them the initial benefit of the doubt, but I'd probe quickly for some job-related specifics.

☞ *Lack of enthusiasm.* If they aren't excited about interviewing for the job, why do you think they'll suddenly "get religion" when you hire them?

☞ *Nervousness.* Some people are naturally nervous in the artificial and intimidating atmosphere of an interview (even one with a sweetheart like you), so I wouldn't consider this an automatic reason to have your secretary buzz you about that "emergency conference." But it could be a harbinger that something is lurking—a firing, a sexual harassment suit, *some*thing that isn't going to make your day. Try to make the atmosphere less formal than usual: smile, put them at ease—and see what develops.

☞ *Even if they have solid experience, their skills don't match your needs.* I'm always amazed at how many interviewers believe that an interview must last a certain amount of time (20 minutes, half an hour, an hour) when it's apparent *in the first three minutes* that the candidate is over-qualified, under-qualified, or "mis-qualified" for the job they're trying to fill. There is nothing wrong with continuing the interview to ascertain whether he or she is a good candidate for another (even future) opening. Or a future opening. But don't kid yourself—this candidate is not right for *you now!*

☞ *Someone who asks a clarifying question,* such as "What exactly do you want to know?" or "Which particular areas would you like me to talk about?"

As I said earlier, I find it hard to believe anyone interviewing for anything has not anticipated that this question will be asked. What does he *think* you want to know? His opinion about Michael Jordan's retirement? You want to know about his experience, skills, talents, and education, and if he can't figure that out, you shouldn't go any further.

Variations

☞ *What makes you special (unique, different)?*

☞ *What five adjectives describe you best?*

☞ *Rate yourself on a scale of 1 to 10.*

☞ *How would you describe your character?*

☞ *How would you describe your personality?*

Despite the nuances, I wouldn't be surprised if a savvy candidate merely edited his or her "set piece" to respond to each of the above questions in essentially the same way. So although the first fourth and fifth questions appear to be more targeted, all five questions are really looking for the same information:

☞ *Why should I hire you?*

☞ *Why should I consider you a strong candidate for this position?*

☞ *What's better about you than the other candidates I'm interviewing?*

☞ *What can you do for me that someone else can't?*

These are more aggressive questions. While you should be expecting the same information, the tone of each of these questions is a bit more forceful: You're clearly attempting to make candidates fully aware that they're in the hot seat. This may be a matter of your own style, the introduction to your own brand of stress interview, or just a way to save time by seeing how they respond to pressure right from the get-go.

In one respect, I think phrasing your first question this way *helps* the candidate: You've virtually required that her answer match specific strengths, accomplishments, skills, and so on, to job requirements you've already enumerated (in an ad, through personnel, or whatever). You've given her a bit more "direction" than a simple question like "Tell me about yourself" does.

On the other hand, you've immediately given yourself an opportunity to measure the extent (or actual existence) of the pre-interview research the applicant has undertaken and the ability to separate the "mis-qualified" after a single question. The applicant, for example, may emphasize her ability to meet deadlines and cite specific instances, which clearly show she worked virtually alone.

In the position you have available, the successful candidate may have to coddle and cajole a wide variety of managers in several offices across the country to get input for the documents he is then supposed to produce, then he will have to follow through by getting each one to sign off on the finished product. Although "tenacity" and "meeting deadlines" may come trippingly off his tongue, you need a very different—highly diplomatic, team player, and so on—individual.

Q: What are your strengths as an employee?

This is probably helpful to those who haven't prepared as well, as you're giving them the hint you want their experience/ skills to match your needs and don't care about their captaincy of the chess club in junior high. Although it's still an open-ended question, it tends to focus the conversation too early. I prefer not to ask it, certainly not at the very beginning of an interview. The natural follow-up question, and the one some candidates may not be as prepared for, is "Go ahead and tell me about your biggest weaknesses."

Q: How would your (best friend, college roommate, favorite professor, mother, family, favorite boss, and so on) describe you?

Personally, I would start with the "best friend" variation if you're going to use this question. Supposedly, that's who should know the candidate best, so if you get a half-baked picture of the applicant, you'll know you can shorten the interview—by about 7/8 of an hour. Another approach is to ask the applicant to describe his or her best friend and how that friend differs from him or her. Because the candidate is supposedly describing her best friend, not herself, she may offer character insights you wouldn't get otherwise.

All of the other variations on this question can be used to hone in on specific times (college, high school, last job) or just to get a fuller picture of the person. What someone's mother or father would say, for example, will often give you a clear illustration of the kind of environment in which the applicant was raised.

Q: What do you want to be doing five years from now?

What do you want to hear?

Are the candidate's goals and yours compatible? Is he looking for fast or steady growth in a position you know is a virtual dead end? Is she demanding more money than you can ever pay? How have the candidate's goals and motivations changed as he has matured and gained work experience? If she has recently become a manager, how has that change affected her future career outlook? If he has realized he needs to acquire or hone a particular skill, how and when is he planning to do so?

This question is not as popular as it once was, because the pace of change at many corporations continues to increase so rapidly. You are probably more concerned about the candidate's ability to make a more immediate impact, so you may ask something like, "What will you be able to accomplish during your first 90 (100, 180) days on the job"?

Green light

Here's a good general answer, if only because it opens up so many specific areas for follow-up questions:

"That will ultimately depend on my performance on the job, and on the growth and opportunities offered by my employer.

"I've already demonstrated leadership characteristics in all of the jobs I've held, so I'm very confident that I will take on progressively greater management responsibilities in the future. That suits me fine. I enjoy building a team, developing its goals, then working to accomplish those goals."

In other words, she wants "more"—more responsibility, more people reporting to her, more turf, even more money. A general answer (as previously mentioned) is only a starting point—don't fail to ask the obvious follow-up questions (using the answer to the previous question as a guide):

☞ *Tell me about the last team you led.*

☞ *Tell me about the last project your team undertook.*

☞ *What was the most satisfying position you've held, and why?*

☞ *If I told you our growth was phenomenal and you could go as far as your abilities would take you, where would that be, and how quickly?*

 Red light

Anyone answering "your job." Aren't you as tired of that now trite response as I am?

Anyone who offers a "general" answer—that is, no real specific goals—no matter how much you probe. That should be a tip-off that this particular candidate has not taken the time to really think about his future, which makes it impossible for *you* to assess whether there's a "fit" between his goals and yours.

Anyone who says he wants to be in the same job for which he's applying (unless it is a dead-end job and you'd be happy as punch if someone actually stayed longer than three weeks, unlike the last 14 people to hold the position!).

Anyone whose answer reveals unrealistic expectations. A candidate should have some idea of the time it takes to climb the career ladder in your particular industry or even in your company. While someone hoping to go from account manager to CEO in two years should raise an obvious red flag, any expectations that are far too ambitious should give you pause. If a law school grad, for example, seeks to make partner in four years—when the average for all firms is seven and, for yours, 10—doesn't that make you question the extent and effectiveness of her preinterview research?

There's nothing wrong with being ambitious and confident beyond all bounds, but a savvy interviewee should temper such boundless expectations during the interview. We all know that some candidates do successfully "break the rules," but most interviewers get a little nervous around people with completely unbridled ambition!

If you're worried that your company wouldn't be able to deliver on the promises a candidate wants to hear, you can ask a follow-up question: "How soon after you're hired do you think you can contribute to our success?" Even someone with a tremendous amount of pertinent experience knows full well that each company has its own particular ways of doing things and that the learning curve may be days, weeks, or months, depending on circumstances. So any candidate—but especially an overly ambitious young person—who blithely assures you he'll be productive from day one is cause for concern. You're really trying to assess, in the case of an inexperienced person, how "trainable" she is, and she's just told you she thinks she already knows it all! Not a good start.

For some reason, some applicants fail to remember that this is an interview, not a conversation in a bar or with friends. As a result, you may also get some remarkable responses that can only be called "fantasies"—to be retired, own his own business, run an office in Paris—though why they would think any such answer is pertinent to their job search is beyond me. I would seriously discourage employing anyone who answered this question in such a manner.

Variations

☞ *What are your most important long-term goals?*

☞ *Have you recently established any new objectives or goals?*

☞ *What do you want to do with your life?*

Q: If you could change one thing about your personality with a snap of the fingers, what would it be and why?

What do you want to hear?

A smart candidate will take a trait previously (or now) identified as a weakness and put together a brief answer that indicates awareness and motivation:

> *"Boy, I had a hard time with procrastination in college. But I licked it because burning the midnight oil all through exam week every semester was driving me nuts.*
>
> *"I have to confess, I still have the urge to procrastinate. (He or she might smile disingenuously here.) I wish that I never felt like putting things off, because I know what will happen if I do."*

Red light

A candidate who identifies a weakness that is job-related or, worse, essential to the job at hand (for example, an inability to work with others when the job at hand is highly team-based).

Anyone who identifies a weakness that is so basic or stupid that you have to wonder if that's the *biggest* thing (you *did* say *one* thing) they would try to change.

Beware of the unbelievable answer that is just an attempt to skate by the question: "You know, sir, I just work too hard. I have to take more time off than just Sunday from 5 to 7...a.m." Right.

Variations

☞ *Tell me about one thing in your life of which you're proudest.*

☞ *Tell me about the worst decision you ever made.*

☞ *Tell me about one thing in your life of which you're most ashamed.*

☞ *What's your greatest weakness?*

The first question puts the candidate on preferable turf—a positive question he can answer positively. The latter three force him to turn negative questions into a positive answers, and, because any negative question invites the unwary to descend into a sea of recriminations ("Working for that last jerk, let me tell you!"), they are a better test from your standpoint.

In all cases, you're inviting conversation but not as "one way" and open-ended as in earlier questions. These might well be follow-up questions if "Tell me about yourself" or something similar didn't "open everything up" as much as you hoped it would.

Q: Describe your management philosophy.

What do you want to hear?

Someone who can demonstrate a desire and ability to delegate, teach, and distribute work—and credit—fairly (unless, of course, you are an autocratic bastard and seek a mirror image). In general, you probably want neither a dictator nor a pushover. A successful candidate should convey that he has the ability to succeed should opportunity present itself. But he should avoid giving the impression that he's a fire-breathing workaholic ready to succeed no matter what (or who) the cost.

Green light

"More than anything else, I think that management is getting things done through other people. The manager's job is to provide the resources and environment in which people can work effectively. I try to do this by creating teams, judging people solely on the basis of their performance, distributing work fairly, and empowering workers, to the extent possible, to make their own decisions. I've found that this breeds loyalty and inspires hard work."

Red light

One of these answers, all of which I've actually heard during interviews:

"I try to get people to like me so they'll really work hard for me."

"I guess you could say I'm a real people-person."

"I just kind of let things happen and deal with problems as they develop."

"I don't know."

Variation

☛ *Tell me your overall approach to this position.*

I know, I know, it's boring at a time when I emphasized asking open-ended questions that encourage a candidate to talk, but this is too nice a follow-up question to ignore. Besides, it has the added benefit of helping you decide very early in the process whether the candidate is "mis-qualified." Is she a gunslinger ready to clean up Dodge City? A wallflower willing to watch while everyone else joins the dance? Or a candidate smart enough to scout out the lay of the land before rushing headlong into a minefield?

Q: What does "success" mean to you?

What do you want to hear?

A good candidate should offer a balanced answer to this question, citing personal as well as professional examples. If his successes are exclusively job-related, you may wonder if he is little more than an automaton. However, if she goes on and on about her personal goals, you may get the impression she's uncommitted to working for success on the job.

Green light

"I have always enjoyed supervising a design team. In fact, I've discovered that I'm better at working with other designers than designing everything myself. Unlike a lot of the people in my field, I'm also able to relate to the requirements of the manufacturing department.

"So, I guess I'd say success means working with others to come up with efficient designs that can be up on the assembly line quickly. Of course, the financial rewards of managing a department give me the means to travel during my vacations. That's the thing I love most in my personal life."

Red light

- ☛ Incompatibility of his goals and yours.
- ☛ Lack of focus in her answer.
- ☛ Too general an answer, with no examples of what successes have already been achieved.
- ☛ Too many personal examples.
- ☛ Too many job-oriented examples.

Variations

- ☛ *What does "achievement" mean to you?*
- ☛ *What does "challenge" mean to you?*
- ☛ *What does "problem" mean to you?*
- ☛ *What does "impossible" mean to you?*
- ☛ *What does "growth" mean to you?*

Q: What does "failure" mean to you?

What do you want to hear?

A specific example to demonstrate what he or she means by "failure," not a lengthy philosophical discussion more suited to a Bergman film than an interview. This question offers you the opportunity to delve into mistakes and bad decisions, never a happy topic for any interviewee. Look for honesty, a clear analysis of what went wrong, a willingness to admit responsibility (with a small plus if it's obvious they're taking responsibility for some aspects that weren't their fault), and the determination to change what caused it (or examples to show how it's already been transformed).

Green light

"Failure is not getting the job done when I have the means to do so. For example, once I was faced with a huge project. I should have realized at the outset that I didn't have the time. I must have been thinking there were 48 hours in a day! I also didn't have the knowledge I needed to do it correctly. Instead of asking some of the other people in my department for help, I blundered through. That won't ever happen to me again if I can help it!"

Red light

A wishy-washy, non-specific answer that forces you to ask more and more follow-up questions to get some sort of handle on what makes the person tick.

Always remember the point of asking such open-ended questions: to get the candidate talking, hopefully revealing more than he would have if you had asked a more pointed question. So *keep quiet.* Fcel free to nod, smile, or otherwise indicate you haven't fallen asleep. But avoid the temptation to fill those inevitable silences with your own stories. Staying silent during a pause is the most effective way to encourage the candidate to just keep talking—which is exactly what you want him or her to do.

Variations

☞ *What does "achievement" mean to you?*

☞ *What does "challenge" mean to you?*

☞ *What does "problem" mean to you?*

☞ *What does "impossible" mean to you?*

☞ *What does "growth" mean to you?*

CHAPTER FIVE

SCHOOL DAZE

The more jobs a person has had, or the longer he has worked at a single job, the less likely you will (or should) care about what he did in college, let alone high school. As important as particular courses and extracurricular leadership positions may have been a decade ago, no amount of educational success can take the place of solid work experience.

But what about an entry-level candidate with a diploma so fresh the ink could stain your fingers? How do you judge how she'll do on the job when her only (summer) job was intimately involved with salad ingredients? More important, how do you cut through the "creative" resumes that attempt to transform a summer job at the local hot dog stand or on the beach into what sounds like a divisional vice presidency?

I presume you're seeking a well-rounded person who, in addition to getting decent grades, demonstrated desirable traits—leadership, team-building, writing, communicating—either through extracurricular activities, internships, and/or part-time work experience. So be prepared to probe relentlessly to ensure that the glad grad in front of you doesn't cost you six months and thousands of dollars to train—right in time for her to move over to your competitor.

A candidate should list not just a major and minor on his or her resume but pertinent courses as well. And a savvy candidate will ensure that each resume is custom-produced so the particular courses mesh as much as possible with the requirements of the job. The more technical the job, the easier it should be for you to determine whether the candidate has the pertinent training. She either knows C++ programming language or she doesn't. But a liberal arts candidate may have little or no pertinent class work, which means you have to make the connections yourself.

Here are some questions to get you started.

Q: What extracurricular activities were you involved in?

What do you want to hear?

I presume you're seeking a candidate who can demonstrate industriousness, not just someone who did enough to eke by. What the candidate has been doing—*whatever* the candidate has been doing—should show you a pattern that bears at least some passing relation to the job at hand. What he did during his summers, unless it was a pertinent internship or part-time job, is virtually irrelevant. He *chose* a major, courses, activities—you want to know the reasons why he made *those particular choices*. That will be the clearest indication of where his "real" interests lie...no matter what perfect "objective" he's branded onto his resume.

You're seeking enthusiasm, confidence, energy, dependability, honesty; a problem solver; a team player; someone who's willing to work hard to achieve difficult but worthy goals. How has everything this person done in college demonstrated her ability to become your "ideal hire"?

Your particular situation, job, company, and idiosyncrasies will affect how you evaluate campus activities versus community work versus other volunteer activities versus working (especially if the student had to pay or help pay for school). Personally, I like to emulate the draft philosophy of football coach Bill Parcells—always pick the "best athlete," even if he plays a position at which you're already overstocked. (The alternative is to "draft for need," in which you accept a less-qualified player simply because he plays the right position.) Translation of this wandering metaphor: Seek someone who found a way to do it all.

 Green light

Activities that bear some relationship to the job/industry (for example, a college newspaper editor applying for a job in newspaper, book, or magazine publishing).

Activities that show a healthy "well-roundedness." Someone, for example, who participated in one or more sports *and* a cultural club (chess, theater, and so on) *and* a political club *and* who worked part-time, not someone whose focus was solely on a sport or cause, no matter how illustrious her athletic or other achievements.

A candidate who demonstrates the ability to manage multiple priorities (let's not forget course-work and maybe a part-time job here) and good time-management skills. (Unless, of course, you want a single-minded, green-eye-shaded accountant who adds numbers all day and thinks that's just the greatest thing in the world. In that case, look for the guy or gal who was class treasurer and president of the Accounting Club.

(Nobody ever said Bill Gates or his thousands of bleary-eyed computer nerds were exactly well-rounded.) Here's a good answer:

> *"I wish I'd had more time to write for the school paper. Whenever I wasn't studying, I pretty much had to work to pay for college. But I learned a number of things from the jobs I held that most people learn only after they've been in their careers for a while—such as how to work with other people and how to manage my time effectively."*

Red light

Candidates who have spent an inordinate amount of time doing things outside of class but whose GPAs (Grade Point Average) indicate they spent little time concentrating *in* class. (Anything below a "B" average should lead you to ask a whole series of follow-up questions, forcing the candidate to explain "why.")

If a candidate's approach to his or her education doesn't match your needs, it may be a short interview. If, for example, you want even your computer programmers and accountants to be well-rounded, the president of the Accounting Club sporting a perfect 4.0 GPA—with no other jobs, activities, or interests on his resume—might as well be shouting loud and clear that he is Grind City.

Someone who seemingly has tried every activity at least once and has no clear direction. (Why should you assume he'll suddenly change on the job?)

Someone who thinks the perfect answer is a joke: "Well, John, I didn't do much more than drink beer on weekends." I'm probably more appreciative of good jokes than the next guy, but an interview is simply the wrong place and the wrong time to tell them. Even if they're funny, you should question the common sense of anyone who thinks sitting across from your desk applying for a job is a good time and place to test a new stand-up routine.

Variations

☞ *What made you choose those activities?*

☞ *Which ones did you most enjoy? Why?*

☞ *Which ones did you least enjoy? Why?*

☞ *Which ones do you regret not choosing? Why?*

Clearly, there are no right or wrong answers to these questions. You should continue probing in this manner in order to ascertain the way the candidate thinks, how she makes choices and decisions, and how flexible or inflexible she seems to be in her choices. Depending on your own circumstances, you will like or dislike certain aspects of the "impression" these answers will give you, but you can't form an opinion without making the candidate paint the picture!

Q: Why did you choose that college? Why did you choose your major? Why did you choose your minor? Which courses did you like most? Which did you like least?

What do you want to hear?

For someone just exiting college, this series of questions may well be substituted for the ubiquitous "So, tell me about yourself."

If you are interviewing candidates for a highly technical job—engineering, science, programming, and so on—you should reasonably expect that they majored in engineering, chemistry, or computer science, and that their major and even minor coursework is pertinent. If you're lucky, such a candidate will have demonstrated a particular interest in chemistry or computers or mechanical engineering while still in high school, making your task one of evaluating rather than creatively "transferring." (Hmm, that art history course shows analytical skills. Perfect for a computer analyst!)

Though not quite as technical, you bankers and Wall Street types should also have it easy as the Business Administration majors and newly minted MBAs march in with enough statistical and analytical courses to give you more options than Bill Gates would.

If only life were always so easy. More often than not, you will end up spending your days cajoling an endless line of History, English, and French Lit majors to explain how their college education prepared them for a sales/marketing/management/executive position with your firm.

What was the thought process? Did he or she choose a major because it was the easiest? Because it had specific relevance to other interests (demonstrated by consistent volunteer/work/activities)? Because the candidate analyzed the job market and took courses to prepare for a particular career/industry? Just because they were there?

What other majors or minors did he or she consider? And why did he or she choose one and reject the others?

Green light

A candidate who talks about the skills she developed—writing ability, debating and language skills, math—especially in courses she didn't necessarily like or want to take. I *like* to hear that a candidate did well in a course she really didn't care for. It seems to me that a good part of many of my days is spent doing things *I* don't care for, but I still must do them to the best of my ability. Shouldn't you be looking for a new hire with that kind of attitude?

A non-technical candidate who nevertheless can demonstrate job- or career-related coursework.

Answers that deal with the particular courses, not the particular workload or professor's personality.

An acknowledgement that the candidate is well aware that despite his summa cum laude credentials, he probably has less job-related knowledge than the senior person in the mailroom. Humility is an attractive trait at times, especially when it's well-deserved: "Sure, I know this position has its share of unpleasant duties, but I'm sure everyone who's had this job before me has learned a lot by doing them."

 ### Red light

Blaming a professor, even tangentially, for a bad grade or expcrience should give you pause—does this candidate have problems with authority figures?

Complaining about the workload of a course, semester, or year. You are seeking industriousness, not laziness.

There are interviewers out there—and I'm one of them—who go out of their way to describe in excruciating detail the worst or most mind-numbingly boring aspects of the job. A successful candidate shouldn't be fooled into expressing *any* negative reaction (even a raised eyebrow when "garbage detail" is being discussed!).

Variations

☛ *Why did you change majors? Change minors? Drop that course? Add that course?*

Again, what was the thought process? Did the candidate's explanation of why a change was made and the thinking that went into it make sense to you. Or was it simply to eliminate a difficult major for an easier one, a stratagem to take more classes with a girlfriend, or something equally superfluous?

A candidate who has changed majors, perhaps more than once, should readily admit that he simply didn't have all the answers at age 19. (Did any of us?) I suspect you (and many other interviewers) would find such candor refreshing and realistic. After all, how many high school seniors know that eventually they will (or will want to) become accountants or hospital administrators, or loading dock foremen, or, for that matter, interviewers for human resources? But you should expect such interviewees to be ready to show you how their other studies contributed to making them the best candidates for the job.

Q: Why are you applying for a job in a field other than your major?

If the candidate before you is applying for a retail management position, but majored in geology, this is an obvious question. The answer should be brief and positive—she has reexamined her career goals and enjoys customer contact, the competitive nature of sales, and the varied management responsibilities required in retail. And, oh yeah (perhaps with a sheepish grin), there are only 42 new jobs in geology this year—and she didn't get any of them! Are there particular things a geologist must learn that directly translate into retail management? Particular skills? I don't know, but you can certainly ask.

Just because so many students who major in more esoteric areas are, by definition, ill-prepared for some specific jobs, and because many people now change jobs, careers, and even industries more and more, does *not* mean that you cannot and should not put such candidates on the spot. Make them sell you on how their learning will benefit *you*.

Q: If you were starting college tomorrow, what courses would you take?

What do you want to hear?

A bit of candor, but certainly not a dissertation involving a wholesale change of major, courses, and hair color. Maybe he didn't have all the answers at 19, but it would be nice if he knew something.

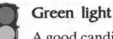 **Green light**

A good candidate should detail changes he would have made in his course selections that would have made him a better candidate for this job. Should he have taken more marketing courses, an accounting course, a statistics seminar? If it's clear to you from the job description that he would have benefited from some such change, it would be nice to hear him state it. He should also not be afraid to admit that it took him awhile to find the right course of study. You've also given him a good opportunity to describe how courses that are completely unrelated to this or any other "real world" career nevertheless were valuable in his development.

 Red light

Anyone who claims they would have gone away to school so that they could date more.

Anyone who answers, *"Same ones, but this time I'd pass."*

Anyone whose answers clearly do not indicate an understanding of the purpose of the question, that is, giving her an opportunity to show she knows what the job entails and would have taken more pertinent courses (while dropping that full-year 17th century Chinese literature course like a hot chopstick).

Q: What did you learn from the internships on your resume?

You, of course, don't really believe that any new hire, especially an entry-level candidate, is going to hit the ground running right out of college or graduate school. Training and experience will be necessary to make him or her productive. So when facing a relatively inexperienced candidate, you should plan to do a bit of probing—trying to determine how "trainable" each candidate appears to be.

 Green light

A candidate who is able to show how the internship experience he has had complements his academic training.

Pertinent internships that tie in directly to his new job/career.

Well-thought-out answers showing career concerns.

Good recommendations from internship supervisors.

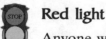 **Red light**

Anyone who sincerely believes—and actually implies to you—that college is where she learned the "Secret of Life." I suspect none of you reading this book would react favorably to someone who acts like she knows it all.

No internships in a field in which they are de rigueur.

Internship(s) in an unrelated field (especially if it ties in with her courses/activities, indicating the candidate's *real* area of interest lies elsewhere).

Poor or no recommendation from his internship supervisor or a negative reaction from the candidate about its value. (Even if his internship turned out to test nothing but his coffee-making skills, a smart interviewee would never introduce such a negative into the interview.)

Variations
- *Why are there no internships on your resume?*
- *Would you repeat each of your internship experiences?*
- *Why did you pick those particular internships?*
- *Why did you feel the need to do an internship?*

Q: In what courses did you get the worst grades? Why? How do you think that will affect your performance on this job?

What do you want to hear?

You should ask to see copies of their college transcripts if they make it past the first hurdle, but in the meantime, you can certainly get a taste of what you'd find there. There may be some surprises in store, like the person applying for that financial assistant job who flunked every accounting course.

Should you expect that every interviewee is a straight-A student and, therefore, will have a hard time answering this question? Not in my world. So the answer to the first part of the question is less important than the explanation and how the interviewee handles introducing a negative ("Yep, I flunked Statistical Analysis, but it was completely outside my major and, as far as I know, has nothing to do with the job you're offering.")

Green light

Anyone who really can't answer the question because they didn't get any bad grades! (Please send them over to me first. I'll take care of them.)

An answer that satisfactorily explains the one or two less-than-stellar grades. If the poor grade was in an elective course, a smart candidate will blame the extra time he spent on his major (in which, of course, he did great). If in a single major course, perhaps outside activities were to blame (and the candidate explains the reasons for placing such activities ahead of good grades).

Red light

Too many Cs and Ds to count.

No reasonable explanation, leading you to assume that the candidate simply didn't care or isn't all that bright.

A choice that the candidate made whose wisdom you question. Although it may have been quite exciting and educational to devote a significant amount of time to getting a friend elected class president, are a plethora of Ds a viable tradeoff?

Variations

- ☞ *Are grades a good measure of ability?*
- ☞ *Why didn't you get better grades?*
- ☞ *Why are your grades so erratic?*

☛ *What happened that semester (year) when your*
   grades sank?

Again, if the student's grades were great, he or she should be suitably proud; if they weren't, hopefully there were mitigating circumstances—work, an unusual opportunity, a family crisis, whatever. If the student fails to take responsibility for a poor performance, consider it a big red light. And if he or she gets defensive, it's the defensiveness you should be worrying about. Did he actually make a choice or simply do something without thinking of the consequences? Pertinent follow-up questions should be obvious based on each student's response.

Chapter Six

Glad You Graduated, Now Tell Me About Your Work Experience

A ll right. You've established your interviewing criteria by considering such important applicant details as college internships and grades. Now the bigger questions need to be asked. The applicant said goodbye to his alma mater some time ago. What has he done out here in the real world?

Q: Tell me about your last three positions. Explain what you did, how you did it, whom you did it with and for, the people you worked for, and the people you worked with.

What do you want to hear?

Whew. This is a question designed to see how well the candidate organizes what could be a lot of data into a brief, coherent overview of three, five, 10, or more years of experience. It will help you to flesh out the resume, catch inconsistencies, create a roadmap for the far more detailed inquiries to follow, and evaluate how well the candidate attempts to "edit" answers in order to relate experience/skills to the job at hand. A prepared candidate may use the well-rehearsed answer to "tell me about yourself" if this question is substituted, which isn't an altogether bad thing for you.

Green light

Pertinent experience and skills.

A candidate who is cognizant of the importance of relating *her* experience/skills to *your* job requirements.

A well-thought-out answer expressed in positive terms.

Brevity.

A clear pattern upward of increased responsibility, authority, money, subordinates, skill level, and so on.

Red light

"What exactly do you want to know?" (Answer: What I just asked for!)

You would think no one would refer to a job that doesn't appear on his or her resume, but it happens all the time. (Follow up: "Your resume says that you were working at ____ during 1996, but you just said you were working at ____? Can you explain?")

Any complaints about bosses, subordinates, and/or coworkers. You're seeking a responsible individual, no matter what the position, so why would you be impressed by anyone attempting to blame everyone else for his failures? Interviewees should know that *even it they weren't at fault*, you're probably not going to consider any transfer of blame a positive.

Lateral moves (why not up?) or, worse, clear demotions.

A candidate's inability to clearly and concisely answer the question and/or to tie all the experiences into a coherent whole.

Q: What was your favorite job? Why?

This is a wonderful question because an unsuspecting candidate will forget to answer it as an interview question and might actually tell the truth:

"My favorite job was at WNSD radio. It was very loose and informal and there was little supervision, which I really enjoyed. I had the freedom to program my own shows with little or no interference and only had to put in 20 hours a week to actually get my work done, so the rest of the time I could write or think up new creative ideas."

Very nice, except she's applying for a secretarial job working for four high-powered businesspeople who are always on deadline and require 10 hours a week overtime at a highly structured and very rigid old-line firm. Thank her and move on!

Green light

An answer that describes a job very much like the one you have open.

A candidate who acknowledges that his favorite job differs from the job at hand in a couple of very specific, perhaps even important ways, but explains why he has changed so that the current job is much better *now* than the favorite job would be.

Red light

Any answer that clearly is at odds with the job at hand. The problem isn't that the last job offered some travel and this one doesn't, or the previous position offered more varied tasks and this one is more highly focused, even if either happens to be the case. The problem for you is that the candidate *failed to take into account what the current job entailed when framing his answer*, which should indicate to you a lack of pre-interview research or the simple inability to realize the importance of matching his past experience to your needs.

A job that's a favorite for frivolous (to you) reasons.

Q: Tell me about the best/worst boss you ever had.

What do you want to hear?

A smart candidate should attempt to describe *you* (as the best one, of course)! After all, that's what you'd *really* like to hear, isn't it? Someone just as wonderful, helpful, motivating, cheerful (brave, clean, reverent, and so on) as *you*. Presuming the candidate is not clairvoyant enough to understand that you expect him to suck up quite that blatantly, at least you should hear that he most enjoyed working for someone who was interested in helping him learn and grow, who was involved in monitoring his progress, and was generous about giving credit when it was due.

Worst boss? Beware the candidate who gets carried away with venomous accusations. They should serve only to introduce doubt about her competence and/or ability to get along with other people.

For example, if she levels the charge of "favoritism," you might wonder (silently or aloud) why her boss liked other employees more than her. If he complains about a boss who was always looking over his shoulder, you might wonder (again, silently or by asking a pertinent follow-up question) whether it was because he couldn't be trusted to complete a task accurately, on budget, on time—or all three? (Which is why he "quit" and is now darkening *your* door, you lucky devil.)

Green light

Any interviewee who sees this question as an opportunity to accentuate her own experiences, accomplishments, and qualities. There are bad bosses out there, but a candidate should be able to put the boss's failures in a positive context. For example, if a previous boss was "stingy with his knowledge," the candidate can accentuate her desire to learn. An "uninvolved" supervisor could be cited by someone who desires to work within a cohesive team.

A "favorite" boss who is close in style and personality to the person for whom the candidate will be working.

Red light

Any negativity.

Any attempt to blame the boss for failures:

"You know, I had to really work hard to learn how to sell spice racks in the South Pacific, but it sure didn't help that my boss had never sold a darn thing to anyone. She seemed to think that everything I did was wrong and constantly called me out of the field for 'evaluations.' I spent so much time filling out unnecessary reports for her and attending meetings to discuss why I wasn't reaching my unrealistic quota that I never had a chance to succeed. I hope my new boss just leaves me alone."

Q: Looking back now, is there anything you could have done to improve your relationship with that supervisor?

Green light

Of course there was (unless the candidate is too dense to grab the lifesaver you've just flung overboard). His subsequent work experience has shown him how to better accept criticism. Now that he has a better understanding of the pressures supervisors are under, he can more successfully anticipate their needs. The successful candidate should grab this opportunity to demonstrate his or her experience, perceptiveness, and maturity.

Red light

"Nah, not with that dumb so-and-so. He reveled in our misery. I'm glad we put sugar in his gas tank!"

Q: What were the most memorable accomplishments at your last job? In your career?

What do you want to hear?

A good answer should focus on the most recent (and, therefore, most relevant) accomplishments, but only those that are relevant to the position for which the candidate is interviewing.

For example, a friend of mine who had been an editor for years answered this question by talking at length about the times she'd been asked to write promotional copy for the marketing department. She was trying to change careers, so she deliberately tried to shift the interviewer's attention from her editing experience to her accomplishments as a marketing copywriter.

A successful candidate should be able to explain why she was able to achieve these peaks in her career. For example:

> *"I really stopped to listen to what my customers wanted, rather than just trying to sell them."*

> *"I realized I needed to know a lot more about Subchapter S corporations, so I enrolled in a tax seminar."*

This type of response tells you the interviewee has given a great deal of thought to how he will reach his realistic goals, rather than blindly plunging ahead in their general direction. By letting you know that she is in the practice of regularly assessing her shortcomings, a savvy candidate shows that she is better able to find the means to overcome them.

Red light

Accomplishments that have nothing to do with the requirements for this job.

Frivolous, meaningless, minor accomplishments:

> *"I finally managed to get out of bed every morning and get to work on time."*

> *"I personally raised $25 for the volunteer fire department."*

> *"I successfully typed all my boss's correspondence the same week it was handed to me, even if I had to work all day."*

Q: What is the biggest failure you've had in your career? What steps have you taken to make sure something like that doesn't happen again?

What do you want to hear?

On the one hand, you're inviting the unwary interviewee to view you as a priest and your office as a confessional, encouraging him to produce a detailed log of his every shortcoming, misstep, and misdeed. Even a modestly intelligent candidate should have learned by now that introducing detailed negativity into an interview does not tend to get one hired.

On the other hand, a candidate can't exactly admit she's never failed at anything (unless she comes from that alternate universe, Planet Perfect), so you're clearly forcing her to at least *introduce* a negative. What you're really looking for is the answer to the second part of the question: "Hey, we've all failed, but what did you do about it the last time you blew it?"

Green light

A failure for which the candidate does not appear to be fully responsible. (When I'm interviewing someone, the way a successful candidate scores the most points is to make it obvious she wasn't fully responsible but is ready to shoulder all the blame anyway.)

A job-related failure, with the candidate convincing you he or she now recognizes what the error was and offering you concrete examples to show how a failure was turned into a success.

Red light

No failure (unless, of course, they show their ID card from Planet Perfect).

A non-work related failure.

No evidence he or she takes responsibility for whatever failure is cited and no evidence that any changes were made as a result.

A candidate who declares "it can never happen again," an unrealistic assessment that calls his judgement into question.

A candidate who actually admits a huge work-related weakness. ("I've always hated my bosses—every one of them. But I think I'll like you!")

Variations

☞ *What's your greatest weakness?*

☞ *What's the worst decision you ever made?*

☞ *What's would you say is the biggest problem you've so far failed to overcome?*

When asking any or all of these questions, you must continually probe, always seeking more and more detail.

If a candidate says his greatest weakness is a fear of delegating because it always seems he can get it done faster/better himself, you might ask, "Tell me about the last time you should have delegated but didn't. What happened? Would you do it that way again? Would you do it differently today?"

Consistent probing—especially when you've asked negative types of questions—may well reveal weaknesses, failures, and problems the candidate would prefer to forget about.

Probing can also help you assess much of the candidate's character: how she reacts to stress; how well she handles pressure, failure, or success; her own standards of "success" and "failure"; how willing she is to assume responsibility, especially for decisions or outcomes that weren't her fault; and so on.

Q: Have you managed people in any of the positions you've held?

What do you want to hear?

Even if you're not hiring this person for a managerial position, I assume you would like to hear a "yes." This would, at the very least, assure you that someone else has trusted the candidate enough to assign some responsibility to him or her, if only for a single, part-time assistant.

Clearly an entry-level candidate answering "no" shouldn't be branded "non-management" material because of a lack of such experience. But I'd give points to any recent graduate smart enough to consider "leadership" and "management" synonymous and lists the clubs and other activities in which she "managed" members or volunteers or built consensus within the group.

If he does have some experience, you will obviously want to know specific details about how many people were supervised and in what capacities they worked.

Green light

Not just management experience, but managing the same (or a slightly higher) number of people in a similarly sized and directed department or division.

A positive appreciation of the varying skills needed to manage and motivate different types of employees, especially if the applicant never actually managed anyone "on the job."

Red light

No management experience for a job that requires they manage people. (Remember, red light means "stop and think," not "stop and leave." If we only hired people who have managed others, how would we ever grow our own stars? And who's to say that outside management experience isn't going to consist of a lot of *bad* management experience?)

Any negative expression of management experience. ("Yes, I managed two people at the last firm and let me tell you, they were both overpaid do-nothings!")

A candidate who appears to underestimate the requirements of management, thinking it's just a move up in position and money but not appreciating the pressures of increased responsibility, new skills needed, and so on, and/or someone who seems unwilling to work to acquire them.

Q: Tell me about the types of people with whom you don't get along.

What do you want to hear?

This is an excellent follow-up question to the previous one, especially if the candidate has indicated great skill at managing and/or motivating people, because it seemingly requires a negative response. This could be a landmine for a candidate who responds too quickly, saying "pushy, abrasive people" only to find out later that you're known for being "brusque."

One person I interviewed gave me what I thought was a good answer to this question:

"I was discussing this problem with my boss just the other day. He told me I'm too impatient with slow performers. He told me that the world is filled with 'C,' rather than 'A' or 'B' people, and I expected them all to be great performers. So, I guess I do have trouble with mediocre and poor workers. I don't expect to ever accept poor work, but I'm learning to be more patient."

Was he *really* discussing this "just the other day?" Did the conversation ever take place? Probably not, but who cares? It's a nice touch! And the answer works, too. Shouldn't anyone you're seeking to hire be impatient with slow performers? He even discussed what he's doing to solve his "problem." Short and sweet, but very much to the point.

Red light

You know the identity of the candidate's boss and with whom he'll be working. If he has trouble with detailed, organized accounting types—a good description of you, his new boss, and everybody you work with—need I say more?

A general, vague answer, supplying little detail—no matter how much you probe or urge—indicates both a lack of analysis and dearth of self-knowledge. Of course, candidates don't really want to answer this question—which is why you asked it—but they certainly should know it and its brethren ("What's your greatest weakness?" "Tell me about your worst boss." "Tell me about your greatest failure.") are potentially on the agenda.

Variation

☛ *What types of people have trouble getting along with you?*

This is a great follow-up question, especially if the answer to the previous question was vague or wishy-washy. You're continuing to probe, and you're not going to stop until you hit a nerve. Even if the answer to the previous question was reasonable, this might uncover some inconsistencies (meaning the candidate anticipated the first question and prepared for it, but was not ready for this corollary question).

Q: Who do you think are our two (or three or five) major competitors?

What do you want to hear?

It doesn't belong in this "group" of questions, but I encourage asking this question (or one like it) as early in the process as possible. It will quickly and painlessly (for you) reveal the depth or shallowness of the candidate's pre-interview research. If the candidate clearly has a picture of your place in the industry and can adequately, even intelligently, discuss your products, their strengths and weaknesses vs. the competition, the health of the industry, and other such topics, at least you've identified a *serious* candidate. Granted, it says absolutely nothing about her particular qualifications for the job, but if she *is* qualified, this display of knowledge may well be that "little extra" that separates her (if only in your mind) from other qualified (even slightly *more* qualified) candidates.

Although a lot of hemming, hawing, and nail-biting—along with an obvious lack of an answer—should not automatically lead to a candidate's dismissal, I would personally consider it a black mark.

Variations

☛ *What's our greatest advantage over our competitors?*

☛ *What's our biggest disadvantage?*

☛ *Which of our new products do you think has the greatest potential for growth?*

☛ *What do you think is the greatest challenge facing our company? Our industry?*

In the world of business, "style" has little to do with how well you dress (although at some companies, and in some positions, the "right" wardrobe may be a defining element of the culture). Typically, your business style is a measure—and often a subjective measure, at that—of how you conduct yourself on the job.

How well do the candidates you're considering get along with superiors? Subordinates? Peers? What's their management philosophy? Do they like to work alone or be part of a team? You want to know how they'll act and interact once they're on the job, and these "style" questions are your informational tickets.

Although you are certainly trying to be as objective as possible in evaluating each candidate you interview, you will undoubtedly base at least some of your hiring decisions on your feelings about each candidate's attitude. In every case, you are assessing how the candidate's style fits in with the organizational culture, your own style and/or the team's style. So, in general, a "green light" is any answer that seems to indicate a positive fit, and a "red light" should accompany any substantive differences of style that you feel may cause problems. For the most part, this makes your assessment of any candidate's answers highly subjective. Rather than characterizing an answer as inherently right or wrong, you are simply trying to ascertain whether he or she will get along with Joe or Sally or Jimmy.

Following is a series of "style" questions.

Q: Are you an organized person?

What do you want to hear?

Even if *you* firmly believe that a neat desk is the sign of a sick mind, you want the candidate to talk in detail about the organizational skills that she has developed—time management, project management, needs assessment, delegation—and how those skills have made her more effective. I'd be wary of a candidate who veers too closely to either extreme—I don't want to hire someone so anal-retentive that he always knows the number of paper clips in his drawer or one so disorganized that I'll be lucky if he remembers it's Monday.

Variations

- *Paint me a mental picture of your current office.*
- *Describe the top of your desk.*
- *Tell me about the first five files in your file cabinet.*
- *Tell me about the first 60 minutes of a typical day.*

Q: Do you manage your time well?

I hope the candidate can truthfully say "yes," that he is a self-starter and (almost) never procrastinates. And, if he *can't* say it truthfully, I hope he's smart enough to realize now is not the time to wail about his broken alarm clock—which is why, by the way, he was 15 minutes late for the interview, remember? Good employees are able to set goals, prioritize tasks, and devote appropriate amounts of time to each of them.

However, in answering a rather conceptual question such as this one (and what could be more conceptual than time?), a savvy candidate should try to sprinkle in specifics. Here are a few examples:

> *"I rarely miss a deadline. When circumstances beyond my control interfere, I make up the time lost as quickly as possible."*

> *"I establish a to-do list first thing in the morning. Then I add to it—and reprioritize tasks, if necessary— as the day goes on."*

> *"I really like interacting with the people I work with. But when I need to focus on detailed tasks, I make sure to set aside time that will be free of interruptions of any kind, so I can work more effectively."*

Q: How do you handle change?

Business is *about* change. In order to remain competitive, we have to adapt to changes in technology, personnel, leadership, business structure, the types of services we deliver, even the products we produce. So you would expect a successful candidate to be flexible, willing and able to adapt.

Only *you* know in detail the kind of changes your company goes through on a weekly or monthly basis. If you are a fast-growing entrepreneurial firm, change is your middle name. Someone otherwise super-qualified but addicted to security and structure will not be a happy camper. A candidate more comfortable in a fast-moving, make-decisions-by-the-seat-of-your-pants kind of atmosphere, might be the right hire even if she is less qualified educationally or experience-wise.

A good candidate should choose an example of a change she faced that resulted in something positive, trying to show that she not only accepted change and adapted to it, but flourished because of it:

> *"My boss recently decided our company needed to develop a virtual storefront on the Web. I was given the task, along with a designer, of taking the project from the research phase to operation in eight weeks. I didn't have any special expertise in the area of computers and online communications, so I have to assume I was given the task because I adapt well.*
>
> *"We researched the subject, examined the alternatives, and presented a plan that was accepted. Then I worked with the designer to present information in a medium neither of us had ever worked with before. In our second month online, sales were up 7 percent over the same time last year."*

Q: How do you go about making important decisions?

Presuming that quite a few questions have already gone by, a good candidate should already have some sense, both from his own research and from the previous questions, of your company's particular culture. He should shade his answer to this question accordingly.

On the other hand, you need to think in terms of your main concerns when evaluating his answer. You know the position for which you are hiring. Will the successful candidate need to be analytical? Creative? Willing to call on the expertise of others? Able to work alone? To travel on a moment's notice?

You might hope to hear something like this:

"When I'm faced with an important decision, I ask the advice of others. I try to consider everything. But ultimately, I'm the one who decides. I guess that's why they say, 'It's lonely at the top.' The higher you go in management, the more responsibility you have and the more decisions you have to make by yourself."

Although this is a nice general answer, you probably want to probe to see if the "rubber meets the road." Ask something like, "So tell me about the last important decision you had to make, how you went about making it, and the results you achieved." Can the candidate match in particulars the nice general answer given previously? Or does she inadvertently show she does things completely differently (better or worse) than she just said she did?

Q: Do you work well under pressure?

You will expect everyone to say "yes" to this question (and probably eliminate anyone foolish enough to say "no"). However, you will probe and make candidates provide examples that support their claims about being the Second Coming of Cool Hand Luke. Be wary of candidates who choose anecdotes that imply that the pressure they've faced has resulted from their own procrastination or failure to anticipate problems.

Variation

☞ *Tell me about the last time pressure led you to in-decision, a poor decision, or a mistake. What would you have done differently? Have you found yourself in a similar situation since? What did you do?*

The questioning pattern I am recommending throughout this book should be apparent by now: Probe, probe, then probe some more. A candidate can only rehearse so many generalizations and remember a limited number of "little white lies." The more detailed the questions, the more likely you will expose any misrepresentations, exaggerations, or omissions. And in doing so, you will continue to add multihued brush strokes to each candidate's portrait.

Q: How well do you anticipate problems?

All managers panic from time to time, if only in their minds. The best learn to protect themselves by looking for problems that might lie around the bend. For example, one sales manager I know had his staff provide reports on both positive and negative budget variances on a weekly basis. By sharing this valuable information with his boss and also with the manufacturing, distribution, and marketing arms of the company, he helped improve product turnover and boost flagging sales. This kind of story is terrific fodder for successful interviews, and the kind of example you should be looking for.

Q: Are you a risk taker?

You are probing for intimations of innovation and creativity. Is she a leader or one of the flock? But you also want to find out whether he might turn into a "loose cannon" who will ignore company policies and be all too ready to lead a fatal cavalry charge.

Probe, probe, probe. Again, this is a highly (company) cultural question. You might personally prefer Stonewall Jackson, CEO, to be leading your troops into battle, but probably not want him to be your Controller. Judge the answer according to the particular position you're trying to fill.

Variation

☛ *Tell me about the last time you took a risk. Was it the right decision? What should you have done differently?*

Q: If you could start your career over again, what would you do differently?

The savvy candidate should quote Paul Anka (via Frank Sinatra): "Regrets? I've had a few. But all in all, too few to mention."

But listen carefully to which regrets are mentioned and what the candidate claims to have learned as a result. Did he leave his first job because he was too impatient for a promotion, only to realize he hadn't learned all he could have? Did she miss the opportunity to specialize in some area or develop a particular expertise?

Green light

"My only regret is that I didn't go in this direction sooner. I started my career in editorial, and I enjoyed that. But once I got into marketing, I found I really loved it. Now, I can't wait to get to work every day."

Red light

"I wish I had never gotten into magazine publishing in the first place. But now I guess I'm stuck. And to think, I could have been editing garden books for FernMoor Press...."

Variation

☞ *What was the biggest mistake you ever made when choosing a job?*

You're essentially asking the same question, but the negative implication makes it tougher for most candidates to handle. You are requesting a negative answer, which most candidates know is to be avoided at all costs.

Q: Do you prefer to work alone or with others?

Again, the position for which you're hiring will dictate how you should expect a candidate to shape his or her answer to this question. Say you're trying to hire an on-the-road sales rep, who may develop an unhealthy crush on his or her rental car but will otherwise interact solely with customers, waitresses, and hotel employees. You won't want to hear that a candidate thrives on her relationships with coworkers and can't imagine working without a lot of interaction.

Even if a candidate does like the interaction at work, she shouldn't try to paint her environment as a bed of roses without thorns. You know the saying: "You can choose your friends, but you can't choose your relatives." That also goes for coworkers.

Every job situation forces us to get along with people we might not choose to socialize with. But we must get along with them and, quite often, for long stretches of time and under difficult circumstances. A successful candidate will confidently talk about how he or she has managed to get along with a wide variety of other people.

Variations

☛ *How do you get along with your superior(s)? With your coworkers? With your subordinates?*

☛ *How much time per week do you spend working alone? Do you think it should be more or less?*

☛ *Do you enjoy doing individual research?*

The answers to these questions should, first of all, bear some relation to the answers to earlier questions about people with whom the candidate has had trouble or who have had trouble getting along with him or her. But this is, again, a highly cultural question, and one in which the requirements of the job define the "rightness" of any answer. If a candidate thrives working alone but you're hiring someone who will always be part of a team, your response is obvious.

Q: How do you handle conflict?

What do you want to hear?

"I really don't get angry with other people very often. I'm usually able to work things out or anticipate problems before they occur. When conflicts can't be avoided, I don't back down. But I certainly do try to be reasonable."

"I've had confrontations with coworkers who weren't holding up their end of a job. I feel that employees owe it to their bosses, customers, and coworkers to do their jobs properly."

Q: How do you behave when you have a problem with a coworker?

What do you want to hear?

"I had to work with a designer who was obstinate about listening to any of my suggestions. He would answer me in monosyllables and then drag his feet before doing anything I requested. Finally I said, 'Look, we're both professionals. Neither of us has the right answer all the time. I have noticed that you don't really like my suggestions. But rather than resist implementing them, why don't we just discuss what you don't like?'

"That worked like a charm. In fact, we eventually became friends."

Variations

☞ *Tell me about the last time you lost your temper.*

☞ *Tell me about the last time you disagreed with your boss. A coworker. A subordinate. What did you do, and what was the result?*

Q: How do you motivate people?

A good answer will note how it "depends on the person," then offer one or two concrete examples. A poor candidate will imply that all people are motivated by the same thing or can be motivated with the same approach, a kind of "one size fits all" philosophy. This also is a good follow-up question to "What is your management philosophy?"

Q: You've changed jobs quite frequently. How do we know you'll stick around?

What do you want to hear?

As you well know, the hiring process is expensive for companies and time-consuming for managers. Job-hoppers only serve to make it a more frequent process, which you probably wish to avoid. So you're seeking someone who can convince you that your company and the position you're offering is his or her very own "Promised Land."

Green light

A successful candidate will probably either:

- Confess that he had some difficulty defining his career goals at first, but now he is quite sure of his direction.

- Convince you that she left previous positions only after realizing that moving on was the only way to increase her responsibilities and broaden her experience.

Sherri had four jobs in the first six years after college graduation. Her clever reply to an interviewer's skepticism about her staying power combines both techniques:

"All through college, I was convinced that I wanted to be a programmer. But after a few months in my first job, I found that I was unhappy. Naturally, I blamed the company and the job. So when an opportunity opened up at Lakeside Bank, I grabbed it. But not long after the initial euphoria wore off, I was unhappy again.

"By this time I'd noticed that I really did enjoy the part of my job that dealt with applications. So when I heard about the job in end-user computing at Safe Invest, I went for it. I learned a lot there, until I hit a 'glass ceiling.' It was a small firm, so there was no place for me to grow.

"I was recruited for the applications position at Deep Pockets Bank, and I got the job because of some of the innovations I'd developed at SI. The work has been terrific. But once again, I find that I'm a one-person department.

"This position offers the opportunity to manage a department and interact with programmers and applications specialists on the cutting edge of technology. Throughout my career, the one thing that has remained constant is my love of learning. This job would give me the chance to learn so much."

Q: You've been with the same organization for_____years. Won't you have a tough time getting used to a new culture, company, atmosphere, and team?

What do you want to hear?

This is the "flip side" of the previous question. Pity the poor candidate: If he's moved around, you question his staying power. If she stuck with a single company, you question her initiative. *C'est la vie.*

During the candidate's stint with his current company, he's probably worked for more than one boss. He may even have

supervised many different types of people in various departments. Certainly he's teamed up with a variety of coworkers.
And from inside his organization, he's had a chance to ob-
serve a wide variety of *other* organizations—competitors, vendors, customers, and so on. He's flexible—and loyal—and
should emphasize to you that this is a valuable combination.

Variation

☛ *You've been with your current employer for only a
short amount of time. Is this an indication that
you'll be moving on from our company shortly?*

By the time you've asked your introductory questions,
questions about high school and college experiences, and these
preliminary "on-the-job" questions, you should certainly have
an idea of whether a candidate is truly viable.

If she has impressed you every step of the way, keep on
reading—there are more questions to make sure you've found
your new hire. If he is clearly wrong for the position, you can
save yourself some time and move on.

If you still don't know, it's time to ask even more detailed
questions. You've invited each candidate to paint you a picture. It's time to see what else this Rembrandt in front of you
really has to offer.

CHAPTER SEVEN

LET'S FOCUS ON SOME SPECIFICS

Now that the generalities have been covered—pesky things such as motivation and the applicant's basic on-the-job attitude—it becomes important to glean even more particular information on a candidate's past performance.

Q: Tell me about the last time you...

- *Made a mistake.*
- *Made a good decision.*
- *Made a poor decision.*
- *Fired someone.*
- *Hired someone.*
- *Were fired or laid off.*
- *Were asked to resign.*
- *Were denied a promotion.*
- *Learned a new skill.*
- *Developed a new expertise.*
- *Failed to complete a project on time.*

☛ *Found a unique solution to a problem.*

☛ *Found a creative solution to a problem.*

☛ *Found a cost-effective solution to a problem.*

☛ *Aimed too high.*

☛ *Aimed too low.*

☛ *Made (or lost) a great sale.*

☛ *Saved the company money.*

☛ *Went over budget.*

☛ *Exceeded your own expectations.*

☛ *Exceeded your boss's expectations.*

☛ *Fell short of your boss's expectations.*

☛ *Had to think on your feet.*

☛ *Had to make an unpopular decision.*

☛ *Had to implement an unpopular decision.*

☛ *Dealt with a difficult boss.*

☛ *Dealt with a difficult customer.*

☛ *Dealt with a difficult coworker.*

☛ *Dealt with a difficult subordinate.*

☛ *Were frustrated at work.*

What do you want to hear?

These are "open-ended" questions like "Tell me about yourself," thus encouraging the candidate to talk but clearly requiring focused, specific answers. Follow-up questions should be obvious based on what the candidate answers initially: "Okay, I understand how the lack of divisional coordination led to the budget shortfall. And you have clearly taken responsibility for your part in the miscommunication. But what did you do to change procedures to ensure it didn't happen again? And, by the way, *did* it happen again?"

Just keep probing and asking for more specifics, more examples, who said what, who did what, what were the results, what would you do differently now, what do you need to change to do better in the future, what *have* you changed, and so on.

 Green light

A *specific* answer to a *specific* question, the more detailed the better. (But be careful: We all tend to believe a story that contains a lot of detail, precisely *because of* the detail.)

An answer to any of the previously listed questions that has a beginning, middle, and end, much like a good story: Here's what happened, here's what I did, here's what I learned.

Some of the questions *require* job-related answers; others may allow for examples chosen from outside activities, perhaps volunteer work, or any part of one's personal life. A savvy candidate will "mix and match" stories and examples to convince you he is well-rounded and actually has a life after 5 p.m.

A candidate who takes appropriate credit for an accomplishment (reducing costs, increasing revenues, a creative solution, a tough sale) but is fair and honest enough to put his own contribution within the context of what his team/organization/boss/assistants did.

A candidate who has been around long enough to make good *and* bad decisions, good *and* bad hires, good and bad *choices*. The breadth of a candidate's exposure to the basic tenets of business is more important to *me*, anyway, than the extent of her experience.

Red light

That "hard-working, self-starting, high-energy" Mr. Generalization who can't furnish you with any actual examples, no matter how many questions you toss him.

A candidate with years of experience in the same job who seems to have enjoyed little exposure to the normal day-to-day vagaries of the world. He hired someone once and they were fine. Never fired anyone. Can't remember the last time he actually had to make a major decision.

A candidate who was seemingly CEO/COO/CFO/Creative Star/Sales Guru—all at the same time. Even if you have a prodigy in your office who would give Mozart pause, she should be savvy enough not to take credit for every success her company achieved in the last decade (especially if she's only been there three years!).

Q: What do you do when you're having trouble...

- *Solving a problem?*
- *With a subordinate?*
- *With a boss?*
- *With your job?*

Q: What do you do when...

- *Things are slow?*
- *Things are hectic?*
- *You're burned out?*
- *You have multiple priorities (family/work/school)?*

Here are more questions as you continue to hone in on how each candidate thinks and acts in reality. Keep probing, keep looking for specifics and examples. You may well have asked about problems with a boss, coworkers, and so on, 10 or 30 minutes before, so this gives you a chance to approach the same issue from a different direction. The style of question framed along the lines of "What do you do when..." is very different from "Do you have problem with____?"

Q: What are the skills you most need to acquire/develop to advance your career?

What do you want to hear?

A successful candidate should be developing a skill in line with the job you have open, otherwise why is he or she telling you about it?

Q: What do your supervisors tend to criticize most about your performance?

What do you want to hear?

This is another way of framing a series of questions you've probably already asked: What's your greatest weakness? What was your greatest failure? What would your supervisor say about you?

By asking what amounts to the same question three or four different ways, it gives you the ability to look for the inconsistencies that a candidate might well reveal.

Green light

Because I assume you're going to be checking the candidate's references—and contacting his current supervisor after you've made the job offer—an answer that agrees with what the supervisor tells you should be considered quite good. (And you should be able to use the candidate's answer to get a little more information from his ex-boss than he might have been willing to tell you otherwise.)

A candidate smart enough to discuss an evaluation from an earlier job, switching to what she did about it and claiming that her current supervisor would, therefore, not consider it a problem any longer. This is a really beautiful answer from the interviewee's standpoint because it's possible that you can't really check the initial evaluation, which makes the rest of the scenario moot, but it works for the candidate! The way to get around this elegant subterfuge is to follow up with the question: "Was there anything your *current* supervisor criticized you for in your *last* performance evaluation?" Or, "What specific areas did your current supervisor's last evaluation indicate you needed to work on?"

Whatever the answer, if the candidate manages to cite specific and detailed steps he or she is taking to change that behavior, I'd consider it a plus.

 Red light

A candidate who cites a personal quality that might hamper his job performance, such as procrastination, laziness, lack of concentration, a hot temper, or tardiness.

A candidate who claims never to have received a poor evaluation. While not necessarily untrue—there are companies and bosses failing to do systematic evaluations or failing to take them very seriously—it isn't getting you the information you want. So consider the follow-up: "Tell me about the last time your boss criticized you. What was it for? What was your response? What have you done to fix/solve/change what he criticized?" I *would* find it highly suspect for any candidate to claim she has never been called on the carpet for anything.

Q: Did you inaugurate new procedures (systems, policies, and so on) in your previous position? Tell me about them.

What do you want to hear?

Specific, quantifiable results or a good reason why his brilliant ideas (explained in detail, of course) were not implemented. You don't have to be a divisional president or department head to answer this question. An administrative assistant may have creatively and by his own volition instituted a new filing system or used technology to improve a mundane task, like keeping the boss's calendar. You're seeking industriousness, creativity, caring about the organization and its success.

Again, a good answer should include facts and figures—the changes or improvements the candidate was responsible for making and how they helped the company, in terms of increased profits, cost savings, or improved production.

What if she had some good ideas but circumstances didn't allow her company to take advantage of them? Here's a perfectly acceptable answer:

"Sure, we could have expanded our product line, perhaps even doubled it, to take advantage of our superior distribution. But we just didn't have the capital and couldn't get the financing."

Q: Have you been in charge of budgeting, approving expenses, and monitoring departmental progress against financial goals? Are you very qualified in this area?

What do you want to hear?

Financial responsibility signals an employer's faith in someone. Depending on the position you're trying to fill, this may well be a requirement, and the candidate's answer to this single question may be another factor in his hiring or spell instant doom and gloom.

If a candidate hasn't had many—or any—fiscal duties, he should admit it, though nothing is stopping him from creatively framing his reply:

"Well, I've never actually run a department, but I've had to set and meet budgetary goals for several projects I've worked on. In fact, I did this so often that I took a class to learn how to set up and use Microsoft Excel spreadsheets."

If she has had broader responsibilities, you should expect her to talk about her approval authority. What is the largest expenditure she could sign off on? A solid candidate will let you know, in round numbers, the income and expenses of the departments she has supervised.

This question is also designed to trap unwary candidates who lied to the previous question.

If the candidate answers the second question positively, making her a viable contender for the position, here's a good, broad follow-up question: "What are the most common obstacles you've faced when completing assignments or projects on time and on budget? Give me one or two examples and how you dealt with them."

Q: Have you ever fired anyone? Why?

What do you want to hear?

Even if the interviewee had good reason, you and the candidate know that firing someone is never pleasant. She should say so and provide a "sanitized" (and brief!) version of the events. You should expect a modicum of sympathy for the person (people) who got the axe (you don't really want someone who revels in such a role, do you?), an understanding that sometimes people have to be fired, and a readiness to do it appropriately, professionally, and compassionately, when required. A reasonable answer may be:

"Yes, I fired someone who continually fell short of his productivity goals. His shortcomings were documented and discussed with him over a period of months. But in that time he failed to show any real improvement. I had no choice. As a supervisor, I want everyone in my department to work out. Let's face it, though, not everyone is equally dedicated to his or her job."

If a candidate hasn't ever actually fired anyone, you should expect a response like this:

"I've never actually fired anyone myself, but it was the policy at my company that no one could be hired or fired unilaterally. I was asked on two occasions to give my opinion about someone else's performance. It's never easy to be honest about a coworker's

shortcomings. But I felt I had to do what was best for the department and fair to everyone else in it."

Q: Have you ever hired anyone? Why did you choose each of them?

What do you want to hear?

If the candidate has hired one or more people during his or her career, a good answer might go something like this:

"Yes, I have hired people. I have also decided whether some internal applicants were right for jobs in my department. The first time I hired someone, I concentrated on checking off all the right qualifications. I just went down a checklist.

"Since then, though, I've learned that some candidates who became excellent workers didn't necessarily have every qualification on that checklist. They more than make up for what they lacked in the beginning with enthusiasm and a willingness to work with others."

What if he never hired anyone? You should hope he appreciates you're trying to evaluate his management potential as well as his "people" skills and expect an answer like this:

"Not really. But on several occasions I was asked to speak to prospective applicants and offer my opinion. Of course, in those cases, I was trying to determine if that person would be a team player and if he or she would get along with the all of the other people in the department."

If you're hiring at the executive level, most of the previous questions in this book are just as pertinent as if you were hiring a receptionist (although you would expect a different level of answer!). Here are a few questions specifically for that potential CFO, CIO, or Executive Vice President:

☞ *Tell me about the last situation in which you were directed to overhaul a problem unit/department/ division/company.*

☞ *What were you confronted with, what did you do, what kind of culture did you attempt to create?*

☞ *How many people did you hire and fire?*

☞ *What goals did you establish?*

☞ *How long was your outlook and what were the results?*

Pick a detail, either a positive or a negative, and keep probing. You want to get a complete picture of a candidate's:

☞ management philosophy

☞ ability to conceptualize on a general basis and to implement on a specific one

☞ ability to create loyalty, unity, shared goals

☞ ability to create and produce under pressure

☞ ability to stay within budget and/or produce under budget

Variations

☞ *What kinds of decisions are difficult for you to make?*

☞ *How do you going about making a decision?*

☞ *How do you decide which tasks to delegate and to whom?*

Q: How do you "stay in the loop"?

What do you want to hear?

There are many ways to get the information you're seeking with this question. Here are some variations:

☞ *How many meetings do you schedule/attend per week/month?*

☞ *Do you practice MBWA (Management by Walking Around)?*

☞ *Do you spend a lot of time in your subordinates' offices asking questions, or do you prefer to wait for them to come to you with problems?*

All of the previous questions are much more specific than "Explain your management philosophy"—a question an experienced interviewee can wiggle through with a couple of business-guru quotes.

Q: How do you deal with subordinates who are becoming part of the problem rather than part of the solution?

What do you want to hear?

This has been asked previously in other forms. You're trying to separate the real leaders from the "managers with a title" and to ascertain whether this candidate's style will mesh with yours.

Q: See that picture frame on the wall? Sell it to me.

Or the pen, the desk, the paperweight, whatever. I'm not sure I particularly like this question—although it isn't a horrible one to ask entry-level sales candidates.

What do you want to hear?

One of the major characteristics of a truly good salesperson is his or her ability to ask questions and listen to the answers (kind of like a really good interviewer). So a good sales candidate will begin by asking a series of questions about the object and about your particular needs.

An old friend of mine, a sales superstar, once told me that if he asked enough questions, and asked enough of the *right* questions, sooner or later every prospect would tell him exactly what he needed to say to get the sale.

Obviously, the ultimate test of a sales candidate is whether he or she is really capable of selling that object to you. I suspect if you're a sales manager hiring salespeople, you have your own little tests to ascertain whether a candidate has what it takes.

What about the candidate who will have nothing to do with sales? This may still be a viable question if only to see how he reacts under pressure. The less sales-oriented a candidate, the more this question will bother him, making it a reasonable way to put him into a pressure cooker and see if he boils.

Is a fuller picture of that candidate beginning to emerge? Is there a real, live, breathing person in front of you now, rather than the cipher who shook your hand? Good. It's working.

In the next chapter, we'll continue to hone in on the candidate's most current job.

CHAPTER EIGHT

LET'S TALK MORE ABOUT THAT CURRENT (LAST) JOB

Whether the candidate before you has been working for 20 years or 20 days, it is human nature to focus on the most recent job. Even if it boasted the shortest tenure. Even if a previous job was for years and the current one just for months. Why? Because you want to know what the candidate can do for you—right now—and the most current job offers the best available proof.

Q: Why are you thinking of leaving your current job?

What do you want to hear?

Obviously, no one wants to leave a job with which they are completely content (although some people routinely interview to keep "in practice" or stay in touch with what is currently on offer). But the last thing you want is a candidate who heads right for the negative aspects of his current job, or worse, speaks badly about his current employer. It may not be fair to the interviewee, who may well be giving you just the negative "tip of the iceberg" of the Job From Hell, but many of you will assume that, if hired, the candidate will soon be characterizing you and your company in the same disparaging terms.

So a candidate should handle her discontent (if that's what led her here) very gingerly. The less contented she is, the more careful she should be when talking about it. Here's a good answer:

> *"There is a great deal I enjoy about my current job. But my potential for growth in this area is limited at Closely Held, Inc., because of the size of the company and the fact that expansion is not a part of its current strategic plan."*

Green Light

Unless they have been fired or laid off, viable candidates should make it clear that they are sitting in front of you only because they seek more responsibility, a bigger challenge, better opportunities for growth...even more money. *Not* because they are desperate to put some distance between themselves and their current job situation.

A consistent emphasis on moving "up" rather than just moving "out."

Avoidance of any personal and/or negative comments about coworkers, supervisors, or the current (last) company's policies.

Red Light

The introduction of any negative, no matter how horrible the current job situation. (In fact, the more obviously horrible their job, the more points candidates should score in your eyes for creating an impression of relative contentment.)

A willingness to make a lateral move or even take a demotion just to leave the current company, unless the candidate is moving into an entirely new area or field, such a willingness to move "out" rather than "up," would give me pause. What's he or she hiding? Is this just a last-ditch effort to get out before he's shoved out? And what does such a willingness say about his ability to "tough it out" until the right situation comes along? Is your company just a calmer sea in which he can tread water until the right freighter comes along?

A candidate who admits she lies awake nights fantasizing about calling Joe "No Knees" Buzzano to put a contract out on her current boss.

Variations

☛ *What's hindering your progress at your present firm?*

☛ *Is this the first time you've thought about leaving? What made you stay before?*

Q: Where does your boss think you are now?

What do you want to hear?

It's rare to hear something like, "He thinks I'm interviewing with you so I can leave that hellhole behind and, by the way, he'll be calling you tomorrow to find a job himself." You should expect candidates to be seeing you during their lunch hours, after work, or on a personal or vacation day. If the latter, what a candidate does that day is purely his or her concern, so the boss has not been lied to. I personally don't like to hear that a candidate has taken a sick day to talk with me. It's a white lie, but a lie nonetheless.

Green light

The truth, whatever it is.

A candidate who demonstrates his or her responsibility to a current job by scheduling a breakfast interview or one during a lunch hour or after hours. After all, until he leaves, he is still being paid by his current company for a fair day's work.

Red light

A candidate who has blatantly lied or indicates through body language that the question makes him uncomfortable (implying that he *did* lie).

A candidate who demonstrates little or no loyalty to the company that's still paying the bills, whether that organization is enlightened or despotic.

Q: Are you still employed at the last firm listed on your resume?

What do you want to hear?

You probably know the adage that it's always easier to find a job when you already have one. It's still true, because many interviewers believe that an employed person is somehow "better" than an unemployed one, even if the latter is more qualified. Being laid off is perceived by many interviewers as a sign of weakness. I even heard one experienced executive recruiter say, "Oh, if she was laid off, there must be something wrong with her. Companies don't ever let really good employees go!" Would that it were true!

But the fact is that massive layoffs, while not as frequent or disruptive as a few years ago, can and do still occur. And many hard-working, loyal individuals who contributed greatly to their companies—and could be significant assets to yours—have to admit they've been laid off. Personally, I have finally succeeded in convincing myself that there is no shame in this status and give a laid-off candidate the same consideration I do anyone else. And I suggest you do likewise.

What if they were fired? Expect them to come clean quickly and smoothly to turn this potential negative into a positive.

Let's consider the case of Nick. A hotel sales manager, he was unfortunate enough to work for a petty tyrant who made a practice of taking Nick and his co-workers to task often, publicly and mercilessly.

One day, Nick finally had it. He blew up at his boss—and was fired on the spot. Later on, he was asked about his employment status in an interview for another hotel sales job. He answered bluntly, "I was fired," but then explained:

> *"My boss and I just didn't get along, and I have to admit I didn't handle the situation well. I certainly understand the importance of call reports and log sheets and other sales management controls. I guess I interpreted some of Joe's quick demands for these things as a lack of trust, and I shouldn't have. I've learned my lesson."*

Green light

A candidate who talks less about why she was terminated and more about what she learned from the experience.

If she was laid off, or, as the British quaintly say, "made redundant," you shouldn't expect her to apologize. You might like to hear something like, "Yes, I was one of 16 people laid off when sales took a slide."

(The previous statement is an easy way out—presuming she was not a member of the sales department or, worse, responsible for a significant portion of the slide!)

Red light

As always, the introduction of any negative. ("Yeah, I was fired because I'm not as young as I used to be. Wait until they see what my old lawyer has to say about age discrimination. I'll make them pay through the nose!")

Firing for cause, especially if the individual refuses to admit responsibility or to detail what steps have been taken to correct the problem. Most interviewers get understandably nervous hiring someone who was fired for stealing, drinking on the job, hitting his boss, or some equally charming offense.

Q: Describe the way your department is organized. Also, what is the title of the person to whom you report? What are his or her exact responsibilities?

What do you want to hear?

If someone has been vastly exaggerating the duties and responsibilities of his current position, this question will send him to a crash landing.

It should clarify what he really does—how can he be doing "X" if he now declares that's his *boss's* main function?—and set up a series of follow-up questions.

Many of you will use such a response as the basis for immediate rejection. I can't make a good case why you shouldn't.

Green light

Duties and responsibilities that match those claimed on the candidate's resume.

Duties and responsibilities commensurate with the job at hand.

An answer that makes sense given the candidate's answers to previous questions about work experience. The more detailed these answers—and the more you've probed to get them—the easier it will be to catch any inconsistencies (at which point you'll want to return to those previous answers and ask why the current one doesn't seem to mesh with them).

A clearly presented explanation of how her department, division, or company is set up, which is consistent with her resume and implies that she has really done what she said she did. You will, of course, check these claims when you call her supervisor for a reference, won't you?

Red light

A hazy, vague explanation that indicates the candidate may be making it all up as he goes along.

Glaring inconsistencies with the resume or previous answers.

Failure to include a key responsibility or job duty that was previously proclaimed, especially if it's one that is important to your job.

An organizational plan that doesn't make sense to you. (The more experience you have at different companies, the more likely you will have been exposed to different structures and management styles, and the more confident you will feel that a structure that seems top heavy or one that gives lower-level staff members an extraordinary amount of freedom doesn't "feel right.") Use your own experience to craft a series of questions that will paint a fast-talking candidate into a corner.

Q: Tell me about your typical day at your current (last) job. How much time do you spend on the phone? In meetings? In one-on-one chats? Working by yourself? Working with your team (or others)?

What do you want to hear?

Again, you're looking for the detail that will "prove" some of the earlier general statements the candidate has made (about responsibilities, duties, even favorite aspects of the job) or show that those statements were disingenuous or perhaps somewhat excessive.

Variations

- *On a typical day, tell me what you do in the first and last hour at work. When do you arrive and leave?*
- *Tell me what specific responsibilities you currently delegate. Are you delegating too many or too few tasks? Why? What's stopping you from changing it?*
- *How many hours per week do you have to work to fulfill your responsibilities?*
- *What's the most important part of your current job (to you)? To your firm?*

Q: How long have you been looking for a job?

What do you want to hear?

Unless someone has been fired or laid off, a candidate should always answer that he has just started looking. Why? Because rightly or wrongly, many interviewers presume that the longer someone's been out there, the less desirable he is to hire. Needless to say, if you have some way of finding out that the candidate in front of you has been looking for a while (perhaps she was recommended by a recruiter who knows her history), the candidate should be prepared to explain why she hasn't received or accepted any offers.

Is this a prejudice you should buy into? If someone's been looking for a month or two or three, is she inherently less desirable than a newly minted *ex*-employee who's still wearing his company T-shirt under his suit? It's unrealistic to expect that everyone who wants a job can find one right away. It's even less realistic not to assume that the most qualified candidates might well be picky and simply be ensuring a proper "fit" with the right company before plunging back into the corporate seas.

Q: Why haven't you received any offers so far?

What do you want to hear?

Presuming the answer to the previous question was *not* "Oh, you're my first interview," you should expect a candidate to claim that she is just as choosy about finding the right job as you are about hiring the right candidate. If she has already fielded an offer or two, you might expect to hear:

"I have had an offer, but the situation was not right for me. I'm especially glad that I didn't accept it, because I now have a shot at landing this position."

This is one of those nice generalizations that can cover up a bucket of sins, but you certainly don't have to accept such an answer at face value. Your next logical question?

Q: Who made you an offer? For what type of position? At what salary?

What do you want to hear?

If the candidate has already lied, you're about to make him wish he hadn't! For one thing, you probably know a great deal about your competitors and which positions they're trying to fill. So if the candidate proffers information you know to be inaccurate, you can be pretty sure there's a secret to uncover and should move ahead with a series of pointed follow-up questions.

Again, some interviewers will take any admission of lying in these circumstances as a "voluntary" offer by the candidate to end the interview!

Asking for a detailed description of the job she turned down may give you some very pertinent information. You will often find that the other job is completely different than the one she's seeking with your company. Shouldn't this be a red flag? After all, if the job for which she's currently interviewing is "perfect"—as she's proclaimed three or four times already—why would she be interested in a very different job at the other company?

Q: If you don't leave your current job, what will happen there? How far do you expect to advance?

What do you want to hear?

Even if the candidate would rather hawk peanuts at the stadium than stay another month at ABC Widget, he should seek to convince you that he is the type of employee who is capable of making the most of any situation, even an untenable employment situation. He could say:

> *"Naturally I'm interested in this job and have been thinking about leaving ABC. However, my supervisors think highly of me, and I expect that one day other opportunities will open up for me at the company. I'm one of ABC's top salespeople. I have seen other people performing at similar levels advance to management positions. That's what I'm looking for right now."*

 ### Green light

A candidate who claims she will still advance and be given more responsibility, but perhaps at too slow a pace or without adequate compensation.

A situation in which the company, through little or no fault of the candidate's, will clearly not be able to keep or pay its top people what they're worth (for example: a pending merger, bankruptcy, cash flow problems, loss of a key customer or product). Clearly, the candidate's reason for leaving is obvious and justifiable and his future there dim, through no fault of his own.

Red light

"Well, I doubt I'll last the week. Old Scrawnynose will probably fire me right after lunch."

This is an answer that indicates problems at the company for which the candidate must bear some responsibility. ("Well, sales are down 10 percent across the board but my territory is down 72 percent. It's not *my* fault so many stores went out of business!")

Q: If you're so happy at your current job, why are you leaving? Will they be surprised?

What do you want to hear?

I think this is a very difficult question for many interviewees to answer. The more positive they have attempted to be (following all that advice from authors prepping *them*) the smaller the corner they've seemingly painted themselves into.

Some candidates know full well their current company will go out of business at any second. Others dread spending another day under a tyrannical boss or need to get out of a job that simply never lived up to its billing. Of course, they've tried to "paper over" any of these negatives. So *now* what do they say?

A winning candidate will take a deep breath and calmly reassure you that she's made the decision to move toward:

- More responsibility.
- More knowledge.
- The wonderful opportunity available at Good Times, Inc.

What about the "Will they be surprised?" follow-up? I think either answer puts the candidate in a box. If they *won't* be surprised, then all of his other answers better confirm that he simply can't advance, can't get the raises he deserves, is truly working for a company on the verge of a nervous breakdown, or something similar. In other words, the situation truly should be wrong for this candidate, and if his supervisor was called (and you will call somewhere along the line, won't you?), he or she would confirm that the candidate is a winner but it's the wrong time, place, boss, company, whatever.

If they *will* be surprised, then it's unlikely the situation itself is untenable (unless the candidate has, admirably, suffered in complete silence for these many months).

Variations

- *What have you had to change about yourself/your skills/your philosophy/your duties to adapt to changes at your current firm?*
- *What would have to change at your current job to make it tenable?*
- *What aspects of your current job were different than you expected when you took it?*

Q: If you have these complaints about your current job/boss/company, and they think so highly of you, why haven't you brought your concerns to their attention?

What do you want to hear?

Again, you are essentially taking the candidate who has attempted to remain highly positive throughout the interview and "hoisting him by his own petard."

"Some problem-solver you are," you're implying. "You can't even talk to your boss about changes that'll make you happier!"

This is a dead-end for many candidates, except for those smart enough to stay positive despite your best efforts to corner them. A winning answer might be like the following:

> *"Grin & Bear It is aware of my desire to move up. But the company is still small. There's really not much they can do about it. The management team is terrific. There's no need right now to add to it, and they are aware of some of the problems this creates in keeping good performers. It's something they openly talk about."*

Variations

☞ *If you could make one comment or suggestion to your current boss, what would it be? Did you do anything of the sort? Why or why not?*

☞ *If you could eliminate one duty/responsibility from your current (last) job, what would it be and why?*

Q: How would your coworkers describe you?

What do you want to hear?

Of course, you would expect that they would describe the candidate as an easygoing person who is a good team player. After all, he or she might proclaim, "A lot more can be accomplished when people gang up on a problem, rather than on each other."

A candidate who has prepared for interviews by making lists of "My strongest skills," "My greatest areas of knowledge,"

"My greatest personality strengths," will simply go over them and let their coworkers and friends describe them accordingly.

Be careful of overly broad descriptions that could be extracted whole from the Scout Handbook. Simply ask for a job-related experience to illustrate each supposed trait.

Green light

Presuming you have your own mental picture of your ideal candidate—and a list of attributes you consider essential—your list and the candidate's should be a good match.

Red light

A description that bears little resemblance to the characteristics and skills required for the job at hand.

The inability to cite specific examples to back up his claims.

Variations

- *What five adjectives would your last supervisor use to describe you?*
- *How effectively did your supervisor conduct his or her appraisals?*
- *How did you do on your most recent performance appraisal?*
- *What were your key strengths and weaknesses mentioned by your supervisor?*
- *How did your last supervisor get the best performance out of you?*
- *What did you say and do the last time you were right and your boss was wrong?*

Q: Give me specific examples of what you did at your current (last) job to increase revenues, reduce costs, be more efficient, save effort, and so on.

What do you want to hear?

This ties into the earlier questions you asked about budgetary responsibility and how the candidate's current department is organized. It's a good idea after asking the first question or two to ask some different questions, *then* return to the subject later. Many candidates, having successfully navigated the shoals of the earlier questions, may be caught in an exaggeration when you return to the question later on rather than following it up immediately.

Q: What do you feel an employer owes an employee?

What do you want to hear?

A smart candidate will avoid getting into a dissertation on the employer's moral, or worse, legal responsibility to employees. Instead, she will try to refocus your attention on her positive outlook. Because detail breeds follow-up questions, this candidate may attempt very short and sweet answers. By continuing to probe, you can, of course, continue to apply the pressure when you get an answer like this:

> *"I think an employer owes its employees opportunity. In my next position, I look forward to the opportunity to run projects profitably."*

It's up to you how much you care to probe, and may well be a function of your particular company. For example, it may be important to you to clarify a candidate's feelings about the information an employer should share with employees, or the size of the raise pool, or your policy of requiring all employees to refrain from smoking. But a good candidate will be able to joust with you:

> *"I hope that my employer will be respectful of me as an employee and of any agreements we may negotiate in the course of business. However, I know that there are times when organizations face tough decisions that may require confidentiality and affect employees. That's business."*

Q: Your supervisor left an assignment in your in-box, then left for the week. You can't reach him and you don't fully understand the assignment. What would you do?

What do you want to hear?

This question is attempting to gauge whether a candidate has an appropriate respect for hierarchy and deadline demands. Alternatively, it may be a way for a more entrepreneurial firm to see whether a candidate is willing to make decisions when forced to, even if, inevitably, mistakes occur.

If there is truly no way to reach the boss or leave a message via voice mail or electronic mail, you'd expect a candidate to suck up the courage to approach the boss's supervisor (in a way, of course, that would not reflect badly on the boss). Because a new hire would not yet be familiar with the company's procedures, it would be reasonable for him to be sure that he understands the assignment before, perhaps, heading off in the wrong direction.

As discussed previously, a winning candidate will spend more time asking questions than offering answers, attempting to make the "hypothetical" more realistic and practical and, therefore, put himself in a position to use his real-life experience to figure out what you're seeking.

You can, of course, make it tougher by asking him to supply the details, which can give you even more insight into the way the candidate thinks and how she approaches complex problems.

Q: The successful candidate for this position will be working with some highly trained individuals who have been with the company for a long time. How will you mesh with them?

What do you want to hear?

A successful candidate should convince you of her eagerness, as the new kid on the block, to learn from her future coworkers. You would expect her to avoid raising any doubts about how they might react to her and to use the opportunity you have given her to humbly chat about how much she needs to learn...even if, in her heart of hearts, she thinks they're probably all a bunch of old fogies and can't wait to get on board and shape them up.

Q: Your supervisor tells you to do something in a way you know is dead wrong. What do you do?

What do you want to hear?

This is a tough question. A careful interviewee may try to slide by:

> *"In a situation like this, even the best employee runs the risk of seeming insubordinate. I would pose my alternative to my supervisor in the most deferential way possible. If he insisted that I was wrong, I guess I'd have to do it his way."*

This answer may be fine if you're hiring a subordinate and work for a company that lives and dies by the chain of command. If you're seeking hot-blooded self-starters, an answer like this may possibly spell doom for an otherwise qualified candidate.

Q: If you were unfairly criticized by your supervisor, what would you do?

What do you want to hear?

All of us can think back to a time when the pressure was on and a mistake was made. Maybe you took more than your fair share of the blame. Perhaps you were caught in circumstances beyond your control. In any event, your boss blamed you. But chances are, you and your boss got through the rough spot and you made sure the mistake never occurred again.

The candidate undoubtedly has gone through a similar situation and should craft an answer that refers to a specific experience. If he's smart, it won't be the most vulnerable or perilous moment of his career. An expected answer may come out like this:

> *"In the course of my career there have been a few times when problems have come up and I have been held accountable for mistakes I did not feel I had caused. But a problem is a problem no matter who creates it, and you certainly don't have to create the problem to solve it. The most important thing is to deal with it.*
>
> *"On those occasions when the issue has been significant enough, I have explained my point of view to my supervisor later—after the situation has been resolved and the atmosphere has calmed."*

Q: Would you like to have your boss's job?

Why or why not?

No matter how someone answers this question, you should learn a lot about her. It's a nice, indirect way of finding out whether or not she wants to be promoted.

Let's start with the first part of the question: A "yes" answer identifies a candidate who is ambitious and interested in career advancement. A "no" indicates doubts or reservations, at least about the job in question.

In the second part of the question, things get sticky for some candidates who have sailed through the earlier stages of the interview. For instance, if it's clear that someone is interested in promotion and the position he is applying for doesn't offer a path to a higher level, then you may well conclude that he'll be disappointed. On the other hand, if you're in a highly competitive organization, you may reject out of hand a candidate who expresses reservations about career advancement.

Green light

Even if you've caught someone totally off guard with this question, the answer better be positive and should tie in to your own culture. It can be as simple as the following examples:

"In time, I would love to have my boss's job. I'm particularly interested in the vendor relationships and sales promotion sides of buying."

"I am very interested in career advancement, but my current boss's responsibilities are heavily weighted toward managing department production. In time, I hope to move into a position with primary responsibility for design quality."

"I would be open to taking on additional responsibilities, but I like the autonomy of a sales position, and I find it rewarding to work directly with clients. My boss is mainly responsible for supervising the department and its personnel. In such a position, I would miss the client contact."

You are in a much better position than I to construct hypothetical situations that will reveal the traits (or their corollaries) you and your company value. Are you looking for creative types ready to take off like a rocket? Or the support personnel who make sure everything's done in triplicate before the rocket is launched? Entrepreneurs ready to plow full speed ahead and damn the torpedoes? Or those who are quite happy to spend their days dotting the "i's" and crossing the "t's", as long as they never rock the boat? The same carefully constructed situations could easily differentiate between such personality types.

CHAPTER NINE

SO WHY US?

Although many candidates ask questions as an interview progresses—and you may or may not encourage such deviations from your formal or informal "script"—it's always a good idea to give all candidates the time to do so. But I strongly urge you to prepare for the detailed questions some candidates will be ready to hurl at you. You may need to research your own company a bit (and think long and hard about the job description) to prepare for the most inquisitive candidates!

Q: Do you know much about our company?

What do you want to hear?

Believe it or not, many candidates think this is merely an icebreaker and simply answer "no." I wouldn't consider this an automatic reason to disqualify an otherwise sterling contender. But I *would* wonder why someone seemingly so captivated by my company and this job (as he's told me, over and over again) would admit to doing no pre-interview research, which indicates to me a total *lack* of interest.

Why would someone go into one of the most important encounters of her life so thoroughly unprepared, and then *admit* it?

A successful candidate should have done her homework and take this wonderful opportunity to show you how *much* homework she has done.

Personally, I would like to hear a few salient (and positive) facts about my company, followed, perhaps, by a question that demonstrates real interest. For example:

> *"Boy, what a growth story Starter Up is! Didn't I read recently that you've had seven straight years of double-digit growth?*
>
> *"I read in your annual report that you're planning to introduce a new line of products in the near future. I jumped at the chance to apply here. Can you tell me a little bit about this division and the position you're interviewing for?"*

Green light

Any answer that demonstrates a candidate's pre-interview research. The more informed he is, the more likely you really are at the top of his list of potential employers.

A detailed answer that indicates the breadth of research, from checking out your Internet site, to reading your annual report and being familiar with your products and services. Referring to a trade magazine article that mentions the company or, better yet, *you*, the interviewer, is a nice touch, don't you think?

Red light

A "no" answer followed by a dull stare.

Variations

- ☞ *What do you know about the community (town, city) in which we're located?*
- ☞ *In which of our offices would you prefer to work?*
- ☞ *Would you have a problem traveling among a few of our offices?*

Following is my own list of questions a candidate should have tried getting the answers to *before* the interview. Notice that I said "tried." Not all such information will be easily obtainable, especially if you're a small, privately held company.

So, as part of *your* preparation, presume that a good candidate will be asking *you* some of these questions:

Questions about your company

- ☞ What are the company's leading products or services? What products or services is it planning to introduce in the near future?
- ☞ What are the company's key markets and are those markets growing?
- ☞ Will the company be entering any new markets in the next couple of years? Which ones and via what kind of distribution channel(s)?
- ☞ What growth rate are you currently anticipating? Will this be accomplished internally or through acquisitions?

- Who owns the company?
- Please tell me about your own tenure with the company.
- How many employees work for the organization? In how many offices? In this office?
- Is the company planning to grow through its acquisitions?
- What has been the company's layoff history in the last five years? Do you anticipate any cutbacks in the near future and, if you do, how will they impact my department or position?
- What major problems or challenges has the company recently faced? How were they addressed? What results do you expect?
- What is the company's share of each of its markets?
- Which other companies serving those markets pose a serious threat?
- Please tell me more about your training programs. Do you offer reimbursement for job-related education? Time off?
- What is your hiring philosophy?
- What are the company's plans and prospects for growth and expansion?
- What are the company's goals in the next few years?
- What do *you* like best about this company? Why?
- What is the company's ranking within the industry? Does this represent a change from where it was a year or a few years ago?

Questions about the department or division

- ☞ Explain the organizational structure of the department and its primary functions and its responsibilities.
- ☞ To whom will I be reporting? To whom does he or she report?
- ☞ With which other departments does this department work most closely?
- ☞ How many people will be working exclusively in this department?
- ☞ What problems is this department facing? What are its current goals and objectives?

Questions about the job

- ☞ What kind of training should I expect and for how long?
- ☞ How many people will be reporting to me?
- ☞ Is relocation an option, a possibility, or an absolute requirement?
- ☞ How did this job become available? Was the previous person promoted? What is their new title? Was the previous person fired? Why?
- ☞ Would I be able to speak with the person who held this job previously?
- ☞ Is a written job description available?
- ☞ Could you describe a typical day in this position?
- ☞ How long has this position been available?
- ☞ How many other candidates have you interviewed? How many more candidates will you be interviewing before you make a decision?

☛ Is there no one from within the organization who is qualified for this position?

☛ Before you're able to reach a hiring decision, how many more interviews should I expect to go through and with whom?

☛ Where will I be working? May I see my office/cubicle/closet/floormat?

☛ How advanced/current is the hardware and software I will be expected to use?

☛ How much day-to-day autonomy will I have?

☛ Does this job usually lead to other positions in the company? Which ones?

☛ Please tell me a little bit about the people with whom I'll be working most closely.

Q: What interests you most about this position? Our company?

What do you want to hear?

You're probably hoping the candidate has his eye on more responsibility, the opportunity to supervise more people and work at a higher level, and the chance to develop a new set of skills and sharpen the ones he's already acquired. And, of course, if you absolutely *insist* you'll increase his salary, well, he certainly isn't one to be negative and say no!

However, this is also the ideal time for a candidate to show what she knows about your company and how the position for which she's interviewing can contribute to its success.

Green light

Again, a successful candidate should have researched as much as possible about your company, the position, even about you, and should take advantage of every opportunity to demonstrate that knowledge to you. A nice answer might be something like: "I've heard so much about your titanium ball bearings that I've wanted to experiment with finding different applications for them," rather than, "I'll have a better commute if I get this job." (Unbelievably, I've heard the latter response from more than one candidate I've interviewed! It may be honest—even very important to the candidate—but it sure wasn't the answer *I* wanted to hear!)

Red light

Any answer that clearly demonstrates incompatibility— if the candidate's primary interest lies in an area that will be peripheral, at best, to his real function, you're just setting him up for a fall. Some previous questions should have identified this "mis-qualified" candidate earlier, but he or she may have successfully slid by—until now.

Variation

☛ *On a scale of one to five, rate your interest in this company. In this job.*

Q: What have you heard about our company that you don't like?

What do you want to hear?

An intelligent candidate will try to minimize negative implications of any question, including this one. If there hasn't been any dire news, you should probably expect to hear about the dearth of the most recent software or the candidate's wish that the company's profits were a bit more predictable. If the candidate raises a huge negative—"I'm not sure I like the fact that I'll be reporting to three different executives" or "Is it possible to be scheduled for a salary review in 30 days?"—one of you has a problem.

Of course, all of this changes if there has been some news that needs to be dealt with. If your company laid off a significant number of workers months ago, it would be reasonable for a candidate to ask if the dust had settled. If rumors of your merger with ABC Widget have been circulating on the Net for minutes, expect Generation Y to know…and ask what the prospects are.

Under normal circumstances, you wouldn't expect a candidate to ask questions like this. But you *have* opened the door and invited them, so I'm presuming you really want to know if there's a hidden objection that may impede your decision.

Q: This is a much larger (smaller) company than you've worked for. How do you feel about that?

What do you want to hear?

If your company is larger, the right candidate is undoubtedly looking forward to terrific growth opportunities and exposure to more areas of knowledge than he or she has access to now.

If your company is smaller, the candidate is looking forward to a far less bureaucratic organization, where decisions can be made much more quickly and where no department is so large that it is not extremely familiar with the workings of the entire company.

Q: What are you looking for in your next job?

What do you want to hear?

Obviously, a savvy interviewee should tailor her response to the job for which she's applying, though answering with a slightly reorganized rendition of the job description isn't the right way to go about it.

Interviewers typically ask a question like this to gauge a candidate's level of interest in the job and see if he has any doubts. A successful candidate should focus on key skills the job requires and emphasize his interest in having a chance to develop (or *further* develop) one of them. Here is an example:

"In my current position as development research associate, I research corporate and government funding opportunities and write grant proposals. I enjoy my work very much, but my contact with prospective donors has been limited.

"I look forward to a position that offers more opportunities to work with donors, securing their support, and insuring that they are recognized for their contributions.

"I have had a few opportunities to do this with my current employer and, based on my success in dealing with Timely Donations, Inc., I know I can successfully advocate an organization's mission to gain the needed corporate support."

Variations

☛ *If you could have any job in the world, what would it be?*

☛ *If you could work for any company in the world, which would it be?*

Q: What aspect of the job I've described appeals to you least?

What do you want to hear?

Let me lead with a little humor. After conversing with his Irish friend one day, a man finally blurted out in consternation, "Why do the Irish always answer a question with a question?" Unruffled, the Irishman winked and replied, "Do we now?"

A heads-up interviewee will do the same:

> *"You've described a position in which I'd be overseeing some extraordinary levels of output. What sort of quality control procedures does this company have? Will I be able to consult with in-house specialists?"*

Much like the question asked earlier ("What have you heard about our company that you don't like?"), I'm presuming you're asking this question to *invite* a real answer. If the interviewee you like isn't going to take the job (unbeknownst to you) because of what he or she believes to be a fundamental flaw in the job, you, or the company, you want to know about it, don't you?

One of three possible solutions will result:

1. You'll discover an objection that isn't valid. Once you answer it, you will again have an interested candidate.

2. You'll uncover a viable objection that leads you to eliminate the candidate from consideration.

3. You'll uncover a viable objection that will lead the candidate to remove him- or herself from consideration.

Q: Based on what you know about our industry, how does your ideal job stack up against the description of the job for which you're applying?

What do you want to hear?

A viable candidate should use her knowledge about the industry to formulate a reply that, though perhaps a bit idealistic, doesn't sound unrealistic. Here's an example:

"I know that many accounting firms are deriving more and more of their fee income from consulting services. I'd like a job that combines my cost-accounting knowledge with client consultation and problem solving. Ideally, I'd like to start as part of a team, then eventually head a practice in a specific area, say, cost accounting in manufacturing environments.

"I know this position is in the auditing area and that you hire many of your entry-level people into that department. I must confess I would like this to be a stepping stone to working more in the manufacturing area and, several years down the line, in consulting. I'm sure I don't have the requisite knowledge or experience yet. Is this a position in which I can gain such

experience, and is this a career track that's possible at this firm?"

Q: How will you handle the least interesting or most unpleasant parts of this job?

What do you want to hear?

If you plan to pose this question, you will probably want to build in specific aspects of the position, such as: "You won't always be looking for creative solutions to our clients' tax problems. Most of the time, you'll be churning out returns and making sure you comply with the latest laws. You're aware of that, of course?" And you would expect a positive response like this:

"I'm sure that every job in the accounting field has its routine tasks. They have to be done, too. Doing those tasks is part of the satisfaction of doing the job well. They make the relatively infrequent chances we have to be creative even more satisfying."

Q: You've had little experience with budgeting (sales, management, teams, and so on). How do you intend to learn what you need to know to perform on this job?

What do you want to hear?

Depending on the kind of job opening and the state of employment in your industry or region, you can't assume you will always (or easily) find a candidate with all the pertinent experience you desire.

You may even prefer to "grow" an entry-level person into a professional position. In either case, you will want to be convinced—through deeds, not just words—that a candidate has the wherewithal to learn what they need to within a realistic time frame. Here's a good answer to this question:

"Well, throughout my career, I've proven to be a quick study. For example, when my company's inventory system was computerized, I didn't have the time to go through the training. But the company that supplied the software had developed some computer-based tutorials and training manuals. I studied them and practiced at home. I hope that I'd be able to do something similar to pick up the rudiments of your budgeting system."

The more involved the training, the more you should want to be convinced that a new hire won't just be twiddling his thumbs, complaining that he doesn't know what to do next.

Q: How long do you plan to stay with us?

What do you want to hear?

One answer I *don't* want to hear is "forever," because I simply won't believe it (and I'd wonder about the intelligence of a candidate who thinks I would). You should expect a fairly simple answer along the lines of "as long as I continue to grow, continue to learn, and continue to contribute in ways you feel are valuable."

I'm not sure whether this question will ever give you any useful information, because any candidate saying "oh, a month or two, until I find a job I really like" shouldn't have made it through your screening process (or, for that matter, the first 10 questions of the interview). But if you watch someone very closely when you ask this question, I've found that body language will often give you just the information you require! Squirming does seem to mean "oh, a month or two, until I find a job I really like!"

If the candidate already appears to be a job-hopper but gives you the standard "as long as I continue to grow, etc.," speech, ask, "Is that what you told the interviewers at your four previous positions?" It will be interesting to see how he or she responds, especially if the answer is, "Yep, and they all believed me, too!"

Q: How do you think I've handled this interview?

What do you want to hear?

Well, now, what is the poor candidate to do? Saying "lousy" doesn't seem appropriate, but "great, sir, and may I polish your shoes?" seems a bit too obsequious. There is no right answer, but it will be interesting to see how much he squirms and how rapidly, if he's really good, he tries to ask a question of his own to get you off this track.

Of course, if a candidate has already decided she's not interested in the job, you might hear some criticisms that will actually make you a better interviewer. So I would only ask this question if you really wanted to hear an honest answer!

You should be very close to separating the wheat from the chaff—the candidates you want to hire versus those you should have sent home an hour ago. In the next chapter, we'll ask the final "wrap up" questions, many of which you may want to intersperse much earlier in the interview process (and I'll tell you why).

Chapter Ten

Wrapping Things Up

Some of the questions in this chapter will be viewed by a segment of candidates as "throwaways," the answers to which are, for the most part, unimportant.

I don't believe in "throwaways," and I think every answer tells a story or reveals another aspect of a candidate's personality or thinking processes.

So some of these questions, while seemingly innocent, may well give you insights that the tougher questions didn't. Although they're near the end of this book, they certainly don't have to come at the end of the interview.

Many interviewers use these questions as "icebreakers," believing that they give a false, informal impression of "let's just chat, shall we?" and lead candidates to drop their interview guard. Some interviewees, dismissed after only a few minutes, belatedly discover that these innocent questions "ice-picked" their chance for the job.

Other questions, primarily those regarding an applicant's health, willingness to travel or relocate, or availability, may be so important to the job at hand that they are near the top of the list of the questions you ask during the first five minutes of every interview. The more important relocation or travel is, for example, the earlier I would ask those questions in the interview (because a negative answer may end the interview then and there).

Q: Are you in good health? What do you do to stay in shape?

What do you want to hear?

You and your company probably have more than a passing interest in your employees' health. Most companies are looking for ways to keep the overall cost of health insurance from skyrocketing. Most managers want to know that a new hire won't be felled by every flu bug that makes the rounds—and on sick leave when they need her most. In fact, many employers make job offers contingent on a candidate's passing a physical examination.

You shouldn't expect (or necessarily want) an exercise nut or someone ready to participate in a triathalon, but probably want to hear that a candidate regularly participates in an activity that provides at least some health benefit, such as yard work, home repairs, even walking the dog.

Q: Do you have any physical problems that may limit your ability to perform this job?

What do you want to hear?

The key words are "ability to perform this job." A physical problem that is *not* job-related is *not* pertinent—and none of your business, by law.

However, I have gotten conflicting advice about asking this question at all. One employment lawyer said that according to his interpretation of the Americans with Disability Act (ADA), even if a disability would inhibit an individual from performing a specific job, you can't ask about the disability. Two other attorneys I checked with said this was hogwash. I would play it safe and check with your own employment lawyer before asking this question.

If you do ask it, you obviously want to hear a simple "no."

Red light

Any question by the candidate as to whether a particular disability would disqualify them, especially if it clearly is a chronic problem for which *you* may soon be assuming liability. "Well, I hope all that heavy lifting won't make me have a fourth back operation" may give you pause. Be very careful how you handle the rest of this interview to forestall any potential discrimination claims. Check with your attorney or legal department immediately.

Q: How do you manage to balance career and family?

What do you want to hear?

Again, this is a perfectly legal question, but it does make it decidedly difficult for a candidate who is determined to keep any discussion of family out of the interview. Why would she want to avoid such a discussion? She may worry that you have some unwritten rules, such as no single parents hired for travel positions (or, for that matter, no parents if travel is excessive), and she doesn't want to lose the chance at the job because of them.

Accordingly, a candidate attempting to give an answer that is as unrevealing as possible may try something like this:

> *"I have been a dedicated, loyal, and hard-working employee throughout my career and nothing in my personal life—family obligations, hobbies, or volunteer work—has ever affected my performance. Nor would I ever expect it to."*

Q: Are you willing to travel?

What do you want to hear?

Presuming he has yet to ask about the travel inherent in the job (perhaps there's none!), you still want to hear something like:

> *"Yes, of course. My family understands the demands of my career and is supportive when I need to spend some time away from home. Approximately how many days per month would I be required to be on the road?"*

While not too many people relish being on the road three weeks out of four, such a schedule is inherent in some jobs and whomever is interviewing for them should certainly be prepared for those travel requirements.

The more travel is inherent to the job you have open, the more likely I would ask this question *early* in the process. Unless you have a good screening process, you may well get the occasional applicant who considers a day a month "excessive travel"—and you need a rep who's out four days a week. (What is he doing interviewing for a job that was advertised as requiring extensive travel? Why is the sky blue?)

Q: Are you willing to relocate?

What do you want to hear?

I presume you're only asking this question if relocation is a clear and immediate necessity (or, at the very least, a real possibility within a year or two), a positive answer is called for. If you revealed this fact in an ad or announcement for the position, you could expect a pretty enthusiastic response— "Absolutely. In fact, I would look forward to the chance to live elsewhere and experience a different lifestyle and meet new people"—unless yet another applicant has decided that "requirements" in your ads somehow don't apply to them.

If you've surprised someone with the news, you should expect a more restrained (but still relatively positive) reply: "Well, not unless the job is so terrific that it would be worth uprooting my family and leaving my relatives and friends. Does this position require a move? I'm obviously very interested in it, so I might consider relocating."

Variation
☞ *Do you have any location preferences?*

Q: What do you like to do when you're not at work?

What do you want to hear?

Many employers subscribe to the theory "If you want something done, give it to a busy person." If you agree, then you will look kindly on a candidate who assures you she is an active, vital, well-rounded individual. You may not get a lot of information from this question: A smart candidate will do everything in his power to remain uncontroversial, citing "reading" and "tennis," for example, rather than "skydiving" or "picketing furriers."

Green light

An individual whose outside interests (or, at least, those being revealed to you) bear some relationship to her career. For example, if you're seeking someone for a position as a bookstore manager, a candidate mentioning that he reads three books a week is highly appropriate. His addiction to helicopter skiing probably isn't (for any job!).

Activities that show the candidate is community-minded and people-oriented—the chamber of commerce, Toastmasters, the Rotary Club, or fundraising for charities.

There should be no problem with a candidate demonstrating an interest in various sports activities—participating in team sports, coaching children, or indulging in activities such as swimming, running, walking or bicycling. It shows he or she is particularly health-conscious, involved, and physically active.

Red light

Couch potatoes: "I'm a Giants fan. I never miss a game. I also catch every episode of *South Park*, *ER*, and *Deadwood*. And I tape my soap operas every afternoon, so I can catch up on them on the weekends."

Those who are so active they are heading for a collapse: "I play racquetball, coach a softball team, am on the board of directors of the local museum, plan to run for city council this fall and, in my spare time, attend lectures on Egyptology at the university." (Whew! How will you find the time and energy for work?)

Those who boast about dangerous activities. "I like to challenge myself. Next week, I'm signed up for another hang-gliding trip. I need something to keep me pumped up until rugby season starts." It wouldn't take much for me to envision a prolonged sick leave on the horizon, a fact that might disqualify (in my mind) an otherwise viable candidate.

A candidate who isn't smart enough to avoid sensitive or controversial topics, especially politics and religion: "I'm always on the front lines at Greenpeace demonstrations." Or "I give all my money to the Crusade to Convert the World to (fill in the blank) religion." If the candidate is a right-wing conservative, how does he know you're not the "last of the red-hot liberals"? And although I noted previously that most sports talk is acceptable, you may wonder about a candidate who talks about hunting or any topic or activity that otherwise reasonable people can still vigorously disagree about.

Variations
- ☞ *What are your hobbies?*
- ☞ *What are your favorite activities in your off-hours?*

Q: What was the last book you read?

What do you want to hear?

You should ask this question if you believe that what someone chooses to read speaks volumes about what kind of a person he is.

Of course, savvy candidates know that, right or wrong, many interviewers seem to think that people who read nonfiction are more interested in the world about them than fiction readers, who they may believe are looking for escape. So rather than talking about the latest thriller they couldn't put down, they will instead quote a popular how-to book they may actually have read (but certainly may not have). Thus you will be told that they're interested in *The Seven Habits of Highly Successful People* or *The Discipline of Market Leaders,* and never admit to knowing Grisham or King or Cornwall.

The more well-read and widely read you are, the more you may choose to make what seemed a simple "throwaway" question into a more detailed conversation about literature, culture, and art. It may have little or nothing to do with your business or the job at hand, but it certainly will give you a better handle on the person sitting before you.

Red light

Anyone who asks "What's a book?"

Anyone who can't remember or admits having read a book—somewhere back in the fourth grade or so.

It's a personal peeve, but is there really a job where reading is not somehow involved? And if there were, wouldn't you still want someone who reads an occasional book, if only a thriller or trashy romance novel? Well, if only a thriller?

Variations

- *Why did you choose that book?*
- *How many books do you read in a month, a year?*
- *What's your favorite book?*
- *Who's your favorite author?*
- *Who's your favorite novelist (that'll teach them)?*
- *What magazines do you read regularly?*
- *Where do you get your news?*

Q: What was the last movie you saw?

What do you want to hear?

Probably not a dissertation about her taste in foreign films or left-wing documentaries or a rhapsody about his collection of *Friday the 13th* movies. Again, who are they outside of work? What do they really like to do? Any glimpse will simply give you one more brush stroke to add to their portraits.

An experienced interviewee will not allow such "conversational" questions to lull him into a false sense of security. He will remember that this is still a job interview, not a meeting of the local literary society or movie fan club. So he will undoubtedly cite a movie that he thinks is what you want to hear rather than the one that accurately reflects his literary or cinematic tastes. But not everyone is experienced and you may get that extra personal glimpse you're seeking.

Variations
- *Who is your favorite actor?*
- *What is your favorite movie?*
- *What is your favorite TV show?*

Q: Do you have any questions?

What do you want to hear?

Presuming that the candidate has already demonstrated some stellar pre-interview research, there should still be other areas to explore. You should expect some or all of the questions noted earlier in Chapter 9 to come up here. And you want them to, because a questioning candidate is probably an interested one.

I will admit it here: I have hired two candidates who answered "No, I don't think so" to this question. I cringed when they said it; I even cringed a little when I then decided to hire them. But they were so qualified otherwise, I discounted that no. However, there were probably some borderline candidates over the years who were sent back to the boondocks solely because they had no questions.

Green light

Questions that are clear, intelligent, and reasonable.

Questions *you* would ask if *you* were being interviewed (which, of course, would make them clear, intelligent, and reasonable, right?).

Red light

"No."

Questions that imply little or no pre-interview research. ("So, what do you guys do?")

Questions that are simply inappropriate, stupid, or unprofessional. ("So, any babes in that department?")

Questions about benefits, vacations, and so on. Although they may well be valid, I don't like to hear them *unless* the candidate has clearly exhausted me with questions about the company, department, and job; *and* it's clear this is the final interview; *and* the candidate is sensitive about asking such questions and couches them carefully; *and* the candidate then moves on to making sure I even want to hire him!

Q: Is there anything else about you I should know?

What do you want to hear?

Even if you're both exhausted, a good candidate will treat this question like a lifeline (and as a sign that you're trying to wrap things up) and, once again, summarize the reasons why he, and only he, is the right one for the job:

"Mr. Krueger, I think we've covered everything. But I want to re-emphasize the key strengths that I would bring to this position:

- ☛ *Experience. The job I'm currently in is quite similar to this one, and I would be excited by the chance to apply what I've learned at BG Industries to working for you.*
- ☛ *Management skills. I run a department almost equal in size to this one. I'm a fair and effective supervisor.*
- ☛ *A record of success. I've won two prestigious industry awards. I would bring that creativity here.*
- ☛ *Enthusiasm. I am very excited about the prospect of working with you here at TCI Ltd. When do you expect to make a decision?"*

Variations

- ☛ *Why should I hire you?*
- ☛ *If you were me, would you hire you?*

Q: What salary are you expecting?

What do you want to hear?

Well, I suspect you'd love to hear something like, "Gosh, this job sounds so gosh-darned wonderful I can't believe you're going to pay me anything! Just give me an office and a phone and I'll work for the sheer fun of it!"

And pigs will be flying to the moon tonight.

This is another question that we've left until the end of the book but you may well want to ask very early on. When I ran a relatively small ($5 million) company, cash flow was a constant nemesis and affording good people was a major challenge. So this question was often the first or second asked by the screening interviewer, because it didn't matter how wonderful the candidate was if he or she wanted twice what we could afford. Even if you've clearly indicated a salary range in an ad, people seem to have no problem asking for double the salary you advertised!

The less leeway you have to adjust salary according to experience, the more likely you want to get this question asked early. But be careful—an experienced interviewee will do everything but jump out the window before being sucked into a salary discussion, knowing full well that his value will increase as the interview goes on.

A successful candidate will avoid committing herself to a specific number and, instead, cite a very broad range: "I believe a fair wage for this kind of position would be something like $30,000 to $40,000." It should be assumed that the bottom end of that range is the minimum salary that the applicant would be willing to accept.

Q: The salary you're asking for is near the top of the range for this job. Why should we pay you this much?

What do you want to hear?

You expect the candidate to justify the higher money, citing all of the factors—accomplishments, experience, skills, and so on—that you should consider before hiring him or her. A candidate may just take an entirely different approach and get "right to the bottom line":

> *"I was able to cut my previous employer's expenses by 10 percent by negotiating better deals with vendors. I think it's reasonable to expect that any additional salary we agree to would be offset by savings I could bring the company."*

Q: When can you start?

What do you want to hear?

If the candidate has been laid off or fired, you would expect him or her to be able to start immediately, of course.

If the candidate is still working for someone else, you would expect him to give at least two weeks' notice to his current employer—more if he is leaving a position in which he has considerable responsibility. (Wouldn't you want that kind of consideration if he were leaving you?)

Because this is the last or very near the last question you might ask, if there is any possibility that the candidate isn't sure, it had better surface now. Just be careful: Do *not* assume that the candidate is ready and willing to go ahead just because he agrees to a start date. If you've been interviewing for any time at all, I'm sure you've had supposed hires, as I have, simply not show up on the agreed-upon start date, without even the courtesy of a phone call. But if you've conducted the interview properly, and use a couple of the closing questions we'll discuss next, you may lessen the odds of staring at a pile of paperwork and an empty desk waiting for your new assistant.

Most interviewees assume, especially if this question has been left to the very end, that they are hired, or at least very close to hired. I suggest you ask this question quite *early* in the process to get some pertinent information right from the start. (You can start tomorrow? What happened to your last position? Only need to give a week's notice? What will your current employer think?)

 Green light

A candidate who says he can't start for three or four weeks because he wants to help his current employer find and train his replacement. It may be longer than you'd like to wait, but I personally would love to be introduced to someone who is that responsible!

If a candidate cannot start for several weeks—whatever the reason—I would consider it a plus if she offered to begin studying literature or files in her off-hours. Or to come into the office in the evening or on a weekend or two to meet members of the staff and begin to familiarize herself with the lay of the land.

Red light

A person who "isn't sure" about when she can start. Because a positive candidate would assume she was going to land the job, why wouldn't she be ready to answer the obvious question about a starting date? As far as I'm concerned, what she isn't saying is that she "isn't sure" about taking the job.

A candidate who can't start for several weeks because he wants to take a vacation. I can empathize with someone who feels the need to "recover" from a bitter job experience before punching the clock at a new one, but there's just something that sticks in my craw about such an answer. Perhaps it's feeling that the new hire is already putting his own needs above mine—maybe it's a real hardship for me to wait four weeks. Maybe it's my own idiosyncrasy, but I *really* hate to hear about someone planning a vacation before starting to work for me.

Q: Is there anything that will inhibit you from taking this job if offered?

What do you want to hear?

"Absolutely not."

You are attempting to do everything in your power to ascertain whether this person will accept the job if offered and actually show up on the start date. But there is no way you can guarantee either. All you can hope to do is give the candidate another opportunity to voice a previously hidden concern— too small a salary, a poor benefits package, a lousy cubicle, reporting to too many people, inadequate support, unrealistic sales or profit expectations, and so on.

Q: Are you considering any other offers right now?

What do you want to hear?

This is another "closing" question I like to ask early in the process so I know what I'm up against. Some of you will want to hear "no," so you feel secure (perhaps unwisely) that the candidate will accept your job if offered. Others will actually welcome a positive response, believing that anyone who is already wanted by other companies—maybe even your competition—is a more attractive candidate.

Of course, this is presuming that you expect an honest answer, which, frankly, I believe is less than likely. Unless he thinks you will respond positively to such an admission, many a candidates will attempt to play their cards very close to the vest. They probably gain nothing by admitting they have other irons in the fire, so why stir up the coals?

Variations

- *Tell me about the other offers you're considering.*
- *How does this job compare to others for which you are interviewing?*

Q: Is there anything in the package I've offered that you feel needs to be discussed?

What do you want to hear?

If a candidate has questions about the reporting structure, workload, or job responsibilities, she will probably feel little compunction to hide her concerns. But money is an issue few people like to talk about. So, even if she feels she's going to be underpaid, she may be loathe to discuss it. Or you may have given the impression that there is little to negotiate. So if the candidate has a slightly better offer in her hip pocket, you may lose her, *even if you would have been willing to increase your offer to beat the competition.* In other words, what you don't know can indeed hurt you, so it is in *your* best interest to give the candidate every opportunity to admit, after much cajoling, that another thousand dollars would lock her up.

You've done it—sifted through the hundreds of resumes, done dozens of telephone screening interviews, brought in six viable candidates for in-person interviews, and finally chosen from them. You know whom you're ready to hire. Now what?

The next step may depend on the type and size of your organization and/or whether you maintain a separate human resources department. But, in general, you will want to phone the candidate to make the offer, give him or her a reasonable amount of time to respond (two to three days is standard, up to a week not unusual) and, presuming he or she takes the job, confirm all pertinent items in writing before the start date.

On page 202 is a rudimentary sample of what such a confirming letter may contain.

Dear Joan:

I'm thrilled that you have accepted our offer to join the team at Wolfsden Associates as assistant actuarial supervisor.

The position pays $45,000 annually, in equal increments every other Friday. In addition, you will receive three weeks' paid vacation, a potential holiday bonus of up to four weeks salary depending upon our attaining company targets, full health benefits (I have enclosed a detailed brochure), and a $50,000 life insurance policy. This position is a three-year agreement, with annual raises of not less than three (3) percent, after which it may be renegotiated. Either party may terminate the agreement upon two weeks' written notice.

I am sure you will be a wonderful addition to our firm and invite you to call me if you have any questions prior to August 15, your agreed-upon start date.

Sincerely,

Jim Dandy
Departmental Head

What about the candidates who didn't make the grade? Because you never know how things will work out in the future—your new hire may last a day, for example—you will want to send a brief but professional letter to each interviewee whom you did not offer to hire. Here's an example:

Dear Ted:

Thank you for applying to American Acme, Inc. I am sorry that we will be unable to offer you the position of Director, Laser Tag Division, for which you recently interviewed.

We have hired another person who had more recent experience. I enjoyed the time we spent talking. I am sure you will ultimately be successful in your job search.

If you should have any questions, please do not hesitate to call me.

Sincerely yours,

Helena Rubenoff
Tag Coordinator

Notice that I did *not* refer to any shortcomings—"We would have loved to hire you but that darn felony conviction got in the way"—nor did I give any details about the person hired. From both a legal and practical standpoint, you have absolutely nothing to gain by including such details.

Besides, *you* don't know whom *Ted* knows. If he left with a good impression of your company—even if the job or company wasn't right for him—he may just recommend an excellent candidate in the future.

If you've asked the right questions, in the right order, and used the information the candidate offered to construct an increasingly detailed array of follow-up questions, you may just have landed the right person for the job.

But let's make sure you don't ask questions that will only land you in hot water. In the next chapter you'll find all the questions you *can't* or *shouldn't* ask, unless the person you want to hire is an employment lawyer.

CHAPTER ELEVEN

STAYING OUT OF THE LEGAL CAULDRON

I f you're a human resources professional, you undoubtedly know every single question you are not allowed to ask of any candidate. And you are probably not reading this book. So let me talk to the rest of you, who may or may not know when you're inviting a lawsuit while you think you're just "making conversation" and getting the interviewee "comfortable."

There are a slew of questions that are simply out of bounds, some of which you probably know, most of which you probably don't. Not every one is patently illegal, but all can be interpreted as evidence of bias if one chooses to do so.

So let's start with the basics—the questions (and variations) you simply must avoid asking. (Specific job requirements may make some otherwise illegal questions perfectly reasonable, so please read the entire chapter!)

Questions about age

- *How old are you?*
- *When were you born?*

☛ *When did you graduate from high school?*

☛ *When did you graduate from college?*

☛ *Are you near retirement age?*

☛ *Aren't you a little young to be seeking a job with this much responsibility?*

☛ *Aren't you a little too old for a fast-changing company such as ours?*

Questions about marital status and family

☛ *Are you single, married, separated, divorced?*

☛ *What do you think caused your divorce?*

☛ *Why have you never married?*

☛ *Were you ever married?*

☛ *Do you intend to marry?*

☛ *Do you live alone?*

☛ *Do you have any children?*

☛ *What was your maiden name?*

☛ *Is that the last name you were born with?*

☛ *Do you prefer to be called Miss, Ms., or Mrs.?*

☛ *Are you a single parent?*

☛ *How many dependents are you responsible for?*

☛ *Who's the boss in your family?*

☛ *What kind of work does your spouse do?*

☛ *How much time do you spend with your family?*

☛ *What do you think makes up a happy marriage?*

☛ *Tell me about your children.*

☛ *Do you have a good relationship with your children?*

☞ *Do you have any children not living with you?*

☞ *Do you live with your parents?*

☞ *What childcare arrangements have you made for your children?*

☞ *My darn kids seem to pick up every bug that comes around. Yours, too?*

☞ *My wife (husband) hates me working on weekends. What about yours?*

☞ *Do you practice birth control?*

☞ *Are you pregnant?*

☞ *Do you intend to have children?*

☞ *Will travel be a burden on your family?*

☞ *Are you a family man (woman)?*

Questions about ethnic origin

☞ *What's your nationality?*

☞ *Hmm, that's a ____ (Italian, Greek, and so on) name, isn't it?*

☞ *What language do you speak at home?*

☞ *Where are your parents from?*

☞ *Where were you born?*

☞ *Where were your parents born?*

☞ *What languages do your parents speak?*

☞ *What do your parents do?*

☞ *Were your parents born in this country?*

☞ *Were you born in this country?*

☞ *What kind of accent is that?*

☞ *What languages do you speak?**

☞ *Are you bilingual?**

* This is a legal question if proficiency in one or more foreign languages is a requirement of the job.

Questions about sexual preference

- ☛ *What's your sexual orientation?*
- ☛ *Are you straight?*
- ☛ *Are you gay?*
- ☛ *Are you a lesbian?*
- ☛ *Do you date other men?*
- ☛ *Do you date other women?*
- ☛ *Do you have any roommates?*
- ☛ *Do you belong to any gay or lesbian groups?*

Questions about religious preference

- ☛ *Are you ___ (Jewish, Christian, Buddhist, and so on)?*
- ☛ *What do you do Sunday mornings?*
- ☛ *Can you work Friday evenings?*
- ☛ *We're a ____ (Christian, Jewish, Muslim) firm. Would that be a problem for you?*
- ☛ *Are you a member of any religious group?*
- ☛ *What religion do you practice?*
- ☛ *What religious group do you belong to?*
- ☛ *Do you tithe?*
- ☛ *Are you "born again"?*
- ☛ *Do your children go to Sunday School?*
- ☛ *Do your children go to Hebrew School?*
- ☛ *Do you sing in the church choir?*

☞ *What church do you belong to?*

☞ *Is there any day of the week on which you can't work?*

☞ *Will working on weekends be a problem for you?*

☞ *What religious holidays will you need to take?*

☞ *What organizations do you belong to?*

Questions about health and disabilities

☞ *Do you have any physical problems?*

☞ *Do you have any health problems?*

☞ *How many days were you sick last year?*

☞ *Do you spend a lot on prescriptions?*

☞ *Can you read the fine print on this form?*

☞ *How's your back?*

☞ *Is your hearing good?*

☞ *Are you physically fit?*

☞ *Were you ever denied health insurance?*

☞ *Were you ever denied life insurance?*

☞ *When were you last in the hospital?*

☞ *When did you last consult a doctor?*

☞ *Do you have a doctor you see regularly?*

☞ *Are you handicapped?*

☞ *Have you ever filed a workman's compensation claim?*

Other personal questions

☞ *Do you own or rent your home?*

☞ *What was your record in the military?*

- ☞ *Have you ever gone bankrupt?*
- ☞ *Have you ever been arrested?*
- ☞ *Do you have any outside income?*
- ☞ *Do you earn any money from hobbies or investments?*

Whew! It's getting awfully hard to get that personal information you want, isn't it? Well, you might want it, but that doesn't mean you can't make good hiring decisions without it. Let's study this problem a little more.

On one hand, as an employer myself, I sympathize with the predicament many of you face, especially if you're with a very small company that can't afford to hire an employee who takes disability leave one month after he or she is hired or wind up hiring someone who has been dismissed from three other jobs for theft.

On the other hand, allowing employers to consider age, marital status, race, national origin, sexual, and religious orientation (as they were able to do when my parents were heading into the workforce) discriminated against 10s of millions of women, Catholics, Jews, African-Americans...and anyone else who didn't happen to be a middle-aged, WASP male.

It may make it harder for you as an employer, but I have to place heavier weight on the side of fairness. So keep trying to find the best person—and stop worrying about what you can't control. That said, you must be aware that there are instances where some of the questions that would otherwise seem biased are perfectly legal and aboveboard. For example, if you're hiring a sales rep who'll be on the road three weeks out of four, it's perfectly legitimate to make a series of inquiries regarding the candidate's feelings about such extensive travel, even about his or her family's feelings.

To be perfectly safe, just make sure you ask *every* candidate these questions. If you are at all unsure whether a question is discriminatory, check with your company's legal department or outside counsel. Given the current nature of our litigious society, "better safe than sorry" might mean "better still-in-business than bankrupt."

INDEX